Inspiration On the Go

INYANG OKUTINYANG

Syncterface
Syncterface Media
London
www.syncterfacemedia.com

Unless otherwise indicated, all Scripture quotations in this book are taken from the New King James Version® of the Holy Bible, Copyright © 1982 by Thomas Nelson, Inc.
(Capitalised text and italics may be used for emphasis)
Used by permission.
All rights reserved.

No part of this book may be reproduced or transmitted in any form or by any means, graphic, electronic, or mechanical, including photocopying, recording, taping or by any information storage or retrieval system, without the permission of the author.

INSPIRATION ON THE GO
ISBN: 978-0-9569741-8-1
Copyright © November 2013
Inyang Okutinyang
All Rights Reserved

Published in the United Kingdom by

**Syncterface Media
London**
www.syncterfacemedia.com
info@syncterfacemedia.com

Cover Design: Syncterface Media, London

Printed in Nigeria by
PRINT.COM
+234 805 340 8426

CONTENTS

FOREWORD	V
ACKNOWLEDGEMENTS	VII
WAKE UP AND GET GOING	9
HOW TO MAKE YOUR GOD-GIVEN DREAM COME TRUE	21
GENERATIONAL CURSES (PART I)	35
GENERATIONAL CURSES (PART II)	47
WHEN THINGS GO FROM BAD TO WORSE	59
TOPPLING THE GIANTS IN YOUR LIFE	69
FREEDOM FROM FEAR	81
WHAT YOU SEE IS WHAT YOU GET	93
WHOSE REPORT WILL YOU BELIEVE?	105
KEEP YOUR MOUTH IN LINE WITH YOUR MIRACLE	117
ARE YOU PASSING YOUR PROSPERITY TEST?	129
PRAISE: THE WAY TO MORE THAN ENOUGH	139
NO MORE CONDEMNATION	151
RUN YOUR RACE	163
THE SALVATION PRAYER	175

FOREWORD

Over the years I have had the privilege of listening to *Revd. Inyang* share from God's word and in my opinion he is one of the *fading few* with the God-given gift of teaching scripture effectively, yet with a child-like simplicity.

I remember listening to him one day and found myself thinking, *"These words really should be inked on the pages of a book."* Well, you can imagine how I felt a few months ago when he told me that he was thinking of publishing his first book. To cut this long story short, today you are holding that book in your hands, and I have the honour of writing this foreword.

Made up of divine snippets from God's Word, *"Inspiration On The Go"* is your perfect companion as its down-to-earth, encouraging content guarantees to help you through the hustle and bustle of each day.

From the first chapter where you are urged to wake up, get into the Word and prayerfully pursue God's will, all the way through to the last, where you find yourself being encouraged to focus on the *prize*, run the race and finish on a high. This book is eye-opening truth all the way and I get the feeling that once you pick it up putting it down will be no easy task!

Each sentence, each paragraph, each page and each chapter simply effuses inspiration and my sincere prayer is that these words will find a place deep within your heart, and ultimately inspire you to become the person who our Heavenly Father has predestined you to be.

Akin Olunloyo
Director
Syncterface, London

ACKNOWLEDGEMENTS

My sincere thanks to Hilary East, for taking the time to work and compile the manuscript which has eventually emerged into the book *"Inspiration On The Go"*

The same and much more to my loving wife, Toyin, for your thorough editorial work in taking the raw material of my thoughts and messages and stitching them together into a truly uplifting book, for the building up of the body of Christ.
You are truly an author's dream!

Chapter One

WAKE UP AND GET GOING

Where are you in your relationship with God? Do you have a way of gauging your position spiritually? Can you tell how much progress you have made in the past year? Do you have a spiritual map that tells you where you are now and where you want to go? It is only when you have identified these reference points that you can make a decision on how you are going to get from where you are to where you want to be. In order to do this you must be spiritually alert and awake. You must be sensitive and obedient to the Holy Spirit.

Hear how the Lord instructs us in the book of Ephesians;

> ...Awake, O sleeper, and arise from the dead, and Christ shall shine (make day dawn) upon you and give you light. Look carefully then how you walk! Live purposefully and worthily and accurately, not as the unwise and witless, but as wise (sensible, intelligent people), making the very most of the time [buying up each opportunity], because the days are evil.
>
> *Ephesians 5:14-16 (AMP)*

In these verses God warns us against spiritual slumber. But how, you may ask, does a person sleep spiritually?

What is spiritual slumber?
"Arise from the dead" implies that when you sleep spiritually you are deadened to the things of God. Rather than being sensitive to the Spirit of life, a *sleeping* Christian is more in tune with the things of the flesh; with carnal and natural activities. Such a person is simply drifting along. They have lost their sense of direction. For example, if you had never been to New York City and wanted to fly an airplane there from Toronto, you would need a map to guide you. However, if you neglected to use the map and just headed in whatever direction the wind was blowing, you would soon end up where you never intended to go! Such is the case of a *drifting* believer. He could even find himself going back to doing those things that he left behind after he was saved.

Spiritual slumber can also be characterized by a lack of spiritual fervour.

> *Never be lacking in zeal, but keep your spiritual fervour, serving the Lord.*
>
> Romans 12:11 (NIV)

It takes sustained effort for us as believers to stay on fire for God, and to keep from succumbing to lethargy and weariness. No one is immune from this danger. That is why Ephesians 5:15 warns us so clearly to be very careful how we live, not as fools, but as wise.

Use the Word to locate yourself
In the book of Matthew chapter 26 we find a good example of victims of spiritual slumber in the eleven disciples when they followed Jesus to the Garden of Gethsemane (the twelfth disciple, Judas Iscariot, had left

to betray Him). If ever there was a time in His ministry when Jesus needed His disciples it was now, just before being arrested and crucified. Jesus knew what was going to happen to Him. After all, that was the reason why He came to earth. But He also knew that His disciples needed to be prepared for what lay ahead:

> Then Jesus said to them, "All of you will be made to stumble because of Me this night, for it is written: 'I will strike the Shepherd, And the sheep of the flock will be scattered.' But after I have been raised, I will go before you to Galilee." Peter answered and said to Him, "Even if all are made to stumble because of You, I will never be made to stumble." ...Peter said to Him, "Even if I have to die with You, I will not deny You!" And so said all the disciples. Then Jesus came with them to a place called Gethsemane, and said to the disciples, "Sit here while I go and pray over there."
>
> Matthew 26: 31-33, 35-36

It was a good thing that Jesus did not depend on these false assurances of loyalty from Peter and the other disciples. If Jesus had depended on the disciples to carry out His mission on earth, humanity would have been doomed! Jesus, the very Word of God Himself, told Peter that before the rooster crowed, he would have denied Him three times and Peter still did not believe it! Obviously, Peter did not have an accurate estimation of his spiritual condition. Not knowing the true state he was in made him overconfident.

An accurate estimation of yourself can only result from seeing yourself through God's eyes - through His Word. Jesus told Peter what his report card was going to be but Peter had an element of pride in him, and could not accept Jesus' words. He assured Jesus that, even if the others fell away, he would not!

Stay awake and pray

And He took with Him Peter and the two sons of Zebedee, and He began to be sorrowful and deeply distressed. Then He said to them, "My soul is exceedingly sorrowful, even to death. Stay here and watch with Me." He went a little farther and fell on His face, and prayed, saying "O My Father, if it is possible, let this cup pass from Me; nevertheless, not as I will, but as You will." Then He came to the disciples and found them sleeping, and said to Peter, "What? Could you not watch with Me one hour? Watch and pray, lest you enter into temptation ('temptation' here means tests, trials and tribulations). The spirit indeed is willing, but the flesh is weak."

Matthew 26:37-41

Here the word 'watch' implies spiritual alertness and vigilance through prayer. Jesus wanted these three men to pray with Him. Often the Holy Spirit will quicken you to do things that your flesh may not want to do. He may ask you to spend more time in prayer, or make some changes in your life. He may tell you to stop doing this, or to do more of that, or even to start making preparations for upcoming changes in your life. If you fail to obey the Holy Spirit's instructions, or if you allow your human reasoning to take over, the result may be disappointment or calamity. For example, do you pray every time the Holy Spirit prompts you to pray for someone? Do you call or visit people when He tells you to? Failure to yield to promptings like these is called spiritual density; insensitivity to the Spirit of God.

From the passage above we learn that we need to pray and get the victory before the testing comes.

If ever there was a time to have His disciples join Him in prayer, it was now. Yet here they were sleeping; even Peter, the very one who not too long before, had told Jesus he was willing to die for Him. Jesus had brought them along to pray, not so much for His sake, but for theirs. It is obvious the kind of spiritual state Peter and the other disciples were in. There is a time to sleep and a time to pray. But their flesh was too weak to enable them to yield to the things of God. Unfortunately, such is the condition of many Christians today. Circumstances always catch them by surprise. They are always asking God, 'Why?', 'When?', 'What?', 'Where?'; never knowing for certain what the will of God is.

Know God's will and pursue it

You are on earth for a purpose. God has called you to do some thing. You have a ministry to fulfill; every believer does. When it comes to seeking, knowing, and fulfilling God's will, Jesus is our perfect example. We need to make the same kind of commitment that Jesus made and always do the Father's will. Jesus prayed in the book of Matthew 26:39, "not as I will, but as You will." He realized that His death, burial and resurrection would be the fulfillment of God's purpose for Him.

There in the Garden of Gethsemane it was evident that Jesus was prepared for everything that was about to happen to Him. He hadn't spent His time hanging around, or shopping, or simply having a good time. Jesus was spiritually in tune every step of the way. He stayed in prayer and He knew exactly what He had been called to do.

> *And Judas, who betrayed Him, also knew the place; for Jesus often met there with His disciples. Then Judas, having received a detachment of troops, and officers from the chief priests and Pharisees, came there with lanterns, torches, and weapons. Jesus therefore, knowing all things that would*

> *come upon Him, went forward and said to them, 'Whom are you seeking?'*
>
> *John 18:2-4*

Jesus had a head start on the devil; there was no way the devil was going to spring a surprise on Jesus!

"Well, that was Jesus" you may say, "How does all that apply to me. After all, I'm not the Son of God." Well, John 16:13 answers that very clearly:

> *However, when He, the Spirit of truth, has come, He will guide you into all truth; for He will not speak on His own authority, but whatever He hears He will speak; and He will tell you things to come.*
>
> *John 16:13*

Now, this does not mean that you will know everything that will happen in the future. But as believers, we should know the things that God has called us to do, and we should fulfill our calling.

There is however a preparatory process that will bring you from where you are to where you ultimately want to get to - to fulfilling God's purpose for your life. The life of Apostle Paul is a good case in point. He had been in ministry for several years before the Holy Spirit said, "separate (or set apart) to Me Barnabas and Saul (Paul) for the work to which I have called them." Paul did not start out by doing what God had called him to do. He started by obeying the Word of God in the book of Ecclesiastes chapter 9 which says;

> *Whatever your hand finds to do, do it with all your might;*
>
> *Ecclesiastes 9:10a*

He continued with that until the Holy Spirit saw it fit to put him into what He had been preparing him to do all along.

Even in the natural, when a five year old child says, "I want to be a doctor when I grow up", he doesn't immediately start taking anatomy and physiology classes, neither does he start examining cadavers. He starts by attending elementary school, then high school, and then he enters the university to begin medical school. It is the same spiritually. If you do not successfully complete all the preliminaries, you will never get to the place of doing the main thing. God will not promote you 'on trial'!

Always be willing

Let us take another look at the passage in the book of Matthew chapter 26:

> Again, a second time, He went away and prayed, saying, "O My Father, if this cup cannot pass away from Me unless I drink it, Your will be done.' And He came and found them asleep again, for their eyes were heavy. So He left them, went away again, and prayed the third time, saying the same words. Then He came to His disciples and said to them, 'Are you still sleeping and resting? Behold, the hour is at hand, and the Son of Man is being betrayed into the hands of sinners. Rise, let us be going. See, My betrayer is at hand.' And while He was still speaking, behold, Judas, one of the twelve, with a great multitude with swords and clubs, came from the chief priests and elders of the people...Then they came and laid hands on Jesus and took Him...Then all the disciples forsook Him and fled."
>
> Matthew 26:42-47, 50, 56

By praying the same thing repeatedly, Jesus was surrendering His will to the Lord. This was a prayer of dedication; it was a prayer of consecration! If you are ever going to do God's will, you are going to have to pray the prayer, 'Not my will, but Your will be done Lord' quite a few times during your lifetime. However, this was the only place in the four Gospel accounts where Jesus actually prayed this way. So do not get the impression that this prayer of consecration is to be prayed indiscriminately in every situation.

For example, we don't pray 'Lord, if it be Your will' I will lead someone to Christ, because we know from the Bible that it is God's will that everyone should be saved. Neither do we pray that way if someone needs healing, because we know from God's Word that it is His will that all should be healed. But when it comes to what God has called you and I to do, which is not expressly written in the Bible, we have to be willing to do whatever it may be that He might ask us to do. You cannot give God preconditions for following Him – "I'll only follow you if..." An attitude like this simply implies that you haven't yet laid everything down at the altar, and you will never be fully satisfied in life until you do.

One young man knew from the time he was saved that God had called him to preach. Unfortunately, he had the unfounded fear that if he ever fully surrendered his life to God, He might send him to China as a missionary. Because he didn't want to go there, he decided not to get too close to the Lord.

As the years passed by, he managed to avoid the call of God, but life was becoming more and more miserable for him. One day, he found himself in a service where the power of God was moving. There he repented of running from God and made a commitment to yield himself fully to His will, even if it meant being sent to China! No sooner than he finished praying that prayer of consecration, he heard the Lord telling him (in what seemed to be an audible voice) that He had never even wanted him to go considered it all to be part of God's plan, and that though they had meant it for evil, God was big enough to have turned everything around for the good of all (Genesis 50: 18-21). Do not make the mistake that so many have made; living with so much anger and bitterness over the things they have suffered. Forgive and forget; release the people who have hurt you and bless them. Then like Joseph, you will open the door for God's blessings into your life.

Before he was reunited with his family, Joseph married in Egypt and had two children:

> And to Joseph were born two sons before the years of famine came, whom Asenath, the daughter of Poti-Pherah priest of On, bore to him. Joseph called the name of the firstborn Manasseh:[a] "For God has made me forget all my toil and all my father's house." And the name of the second he called Ephraim:[b] "For God has caused me to be fruitful in the land of my affliction."

> *Genesis 41:50-52*

Forgetting the painful past enabled Joseph to keep on believing in the dreams God gave him. It enabled him to embrace his future. It is time to forget all your unpleasant experiences. According to Philippians 3:13, you should be " ...*forgetting those things which are behind and reaching forward to those things which are ahead.*" Then your dreams can come true and like Joseph, you too will be fruitful.

How can you tell that some people have not forgotten their painful past? All you have to do is listen to the way they talk about it. You can tell that the wounds are still raw and that they are still feeling the emotional pain. When a wound has healed, a scar remains, but when someone touches the scar, you don't feel the pain anymore. It is important to point out that by forgetting the past, we don't mean to imply amnesia! Of course you will still region such that Jacob had to send Joseph's brothers from Canaan to Egypt to purchase food. Since Pharaoh had put Joseph in charge of all the food distribution, his brothers had to purchase the food from him. Though he recognized them, they did not recognize him, and ended up doing what they had said they would never do when seventeen year old Joseph had shared his dreams with them - **they came and bowed down before Him!** Every last detail of Joseph's dreams came to pass. Not only did he rule over them, they repeatedly bowed down to him - and gladly too!

Forgiveness:
The pathway to dream fulfillment and fruitfulness

It is not hard to imagine the consternation of the brothers when he finally revealed himself to them in the book of Genesis chapter 45:

> *Then Joseph said to his brothers, "I am Joseph; does my father still live?" But his brothers could not answer him, for they were dismayed in his presence. And Joseph said to his brothers, "Please come near to me." So they came near. Then he said: "I am Joseph your brother, whom you sold into Egypt. But now, do not therefore be grieved or angry with yourselves because you sold me here; for God sent me before you to preserve life.*
> *And God sent me before you to preserve a posterity for you in the earth, and to save your lives by a great deliverance. So now it was not you who sent me here, but God; and He has made me a father to Pharaoh, and lord of all his house, and a ruler throughout all the land of Egypt.*

> *Genesis 45: 3-5, 7-8*

Just think about that. Joseph harboured no unforgiveness towards his brothers for what they had done to him, or for all he had suffered as a result of their actions. He the butler was restored to his position of waiting on Pharaoh. In the book of Genesis chapter 41 we read of how two years later, Pharaoh had a very troubling dream that none of his magicians or wise men could interpret. Suddenly the butler remembered Joseph's ability to interpret dreams, and how he had promised Joseph two years ago that he would speak on his behalf to Pharaoh. Pharaoh immediately sent for Joseph, who proceeded to interpret his dream. Pharaoh was so impressed with Joseph that he promoted him to the position of second in command of all Egypt on the spot! **In one day, Joseph went from the jailhouse to the White House!**

Where did he get the wherewithal to be second in command to Pharaoh? In Potiphar's house and the prison, of course! Joseph's move from Potiphar's house to the prison was actually a promotion in disguise; for that was where the Lord perfected his preparation and training to rule a nation!

The process took about thirteen years from the time Joseph first received his dreams to the time of his elevation to ruler of Egypt. All along that long road, Satan was waiting at different stops to steal his dreams and to cause him to give up - through his brothers' hatred, in Potiphar's house, and in prison. At any point along the way, Joseph could have succumbed to anger, bitterness and disillusionment, like many Christians do today. If they only knew what they were throwing away, they would weep for eternity and that still would not be long enough!

Every detail of your dream will be fulfilled
Several years later, we read in the book of Genesis chapter 42 of how there was such a severe famine in the whole

Part of maintaining a godly attitude in the midst of trying circumstances is learning to keep your joy. In Genesis 40:6, Joseph enquired why Pharaoh's chief butler and chief baker should be so sad in prison. One would expect prisoners to have plenty of reasons to be sad! Except if they were prisoners like Joseph, who had tapped into the revelation in Nehemiah 8:10, "....the joy of the Lord is your strength."

Furthermore, Philippians 4:13 says that "I can do all things through Christ who strengthens me." When you lose your joy, you lose your strength and you can do nothing. Someone once said, "If the devil can't steal your joy, he can't keep your goods!" No wonder Joseph was so prosperous. He maintained his joy and therefore his dream, even in the hardest of situations. Though he was in prison, the prison was not in him!

The vision is for an appointed time

For the vision is yet for an appointed time' But at the end it will speak, and it will not lie. Though it tarries, wait for it; Because it will surely come, it will not tarry.

Habakkuk 2:3

Satan may try his best but, when it comes to you, his best will never be good enough. God is at work on your behalf. You must believe that He knows your address, and when He is ready to deliver your promotion, nobody and no demon or devil in hell can stop Him. The Bible tells us that our promotion comes not from the east or from the west or from the south, but from the Lord.

While they had been imprisoned together, Joseph had accurately interpreted some dreams that the chief butler and chief baker had dreamed. Just as he had predicted, like he had jumped from the proverbial frying pan into the fire! What do you do when the dream God gave you seems to get shattered before your very eyes? You put the pieces back together and keep on keeping on! No matter how bad things look or get, there is never a right time to doubt God's faithfulness, or the dream He has given you. When things go from bad to worse, stay faithful to the vision. Believe what God told you, and remain steadfast, unmovable, always abounding in the work of the Lord.

Psalm 105 tells us what Joseph suffered:

> *He sent a man before them - Joseph - who was sold as a slave. They hurt his feet with fetters (or chains), He was laid in irons. Until the time that the word came to pass, Joseph was severely tested and tempted*
>
> *Psalm 105:17-19*

But he passed the test and entered his rest! Do you want to know how to pass your test? Maintain the same kind of attitude that Joseph did. Your attitude is the key to your altitude! Joseph's attitude in prison was such that you would have thought he was in a king's palace. He wasn't blaming God or grumbling and complaining, even though in the natural he seemed to have every right to do so.

The truth is, you just can't keep a good man down. Even in prison, God prospered Joseph to where he ruled over the prison house!

> *But the Lord was with Joseph and showed him mercy, and He gave him favor in the sight of the keeper of the prison. And the keeper of the prison committed to Joseph's hand all the prisoners who were in the prison; whatever they did there, it was his doing. The keeper of the prison did not look into anything that was under Joseph's authority, because the Lord was with him; and whatever he did, the Lord made it prosper.*
>
> *Genesis 39:21-23*

"Look, my master does not know what is with me in the house, and he has committed all that he has to my hand. There is no one greater in this house than I, nor has he kept back anything from me but you, because you are his wife. How then can I do this great wickedness, and sin against God?"

So it was, as she spoke to Joseph day by day, that he did not heed her, to lie with her or to be with her.

Genesis 39: 7-10

Joseph knew that this would not just be a sin against man, but against God. We must never allow anything to hinder our fellowship with God. The devil will bring his temptations repeatedly, seeking to wear down our resistance. Satan didn't succeed with Joseph for he was completely sold out to God. He just kept telling the woman "no". If it is "no" today, it should be "no" tomorrow, and "no" forever!

Let us continue the story:

But it happened about this time, when Joseph went into the house to do his work, and none of the men of the house was inside, that she caught him by his garment, saying, "Lie with me." But he left his garment in her hand, and fled and ran outside.

Genesis 39: 11-12

Joseph did exactly what the Bible says to do with fornication; he fled! Nevertheless, Joseph ended up being thrown in prison after the woman falsely accused him of attempted rape.

Always maintain a right attitude

If some Christians had been able to endure walking in Joseph's shoes thus far, at this point they would have lost it! First, he was sold by his own brothers into slavery, and now he was being wrongfully imprisoned. It seemed

HOW TO MAKE YOUR GOD-GIVEN DREAM COME TRUE | 27

employer coming to you and saying that he knows that the company is being blessed because the Lord's blessing is upon you. What a wonderful witness for Jesus!

Those who are faithful to God's vision will enjoy favour with Him and with others. They will succeed in all their relationships, especially with God. God caused Joseph to be viewed with favour by everyone he served, and that caused him to be blessed in whatever he did. Likewise, the Lord gave Daniel and the other Hebrew children favour and tender love in the sight of all their instructors, and the king of the land to which they had been taken captive. God wants to do the same for us today. We should expect divine favour to work for us at all times. People we deal with will just find themselves liking us, or doing things for us, and they won't even know why. But we will; **it's called favour with God and man!**

Luke 2:52 states that Jesus "increased in wisdom and stature, and in favour with God and men." Many people in the Bible enjoyed favour. If you aren't, maybe you're not believing for it. Experiencing divine favour has nothing to do with your ethnic background, sex, social status, possessions, etc., but with your relationship with God. Ask God for it, receive it and walk in it, for you will need favour to realize the dream that God has given you.

Sin will abort your dream

Joseph's life clearly illustrates the fact that vision restrains people from sin. We need to be careful not to compromise our integrity or obedience to God, especially when the vision seems slow in coming. "And it came to pass after these things that his master's wife cast longing eyes on Joseph, and she said, "Lie with me". But he refused and said to his master's wife...

"Do not give what is holy to the dogs; nor cast your pearls before swine; lest they trample them under their feet, and turn and tear you in pieces."

Matthew 7:6

You need divine favour to fulfill your dream

Now Joseph had been taken down to Egypt. And Potiphar, an officer of Pharaoh, captain of the guard, an Egyptian, bought him from the Ishmaelites who had taken him down there. The Lord was with Joseph, and he was a successful man; and he was in the house of his master the Egyptian. And his master saw that the Lord was with him and that the Lord made all he did to prosper in his hand. So Joseph found favor in his sight, and served him. Then he made him overseer of his house, and all that he had he put under his authority. So it was, from the time that he had made him overseer of his house and all that he had, that the Lord blessed the Egyptian's house for Joseph's sake; and the blessing of the Lord was on all that he had in the house and in the field.

Genesis 39:1-5

Joseph the *slave* is described here as a prosperous man. Some people think of prosperity as having a yacht, a fat bank account, and stocks in the best companies in the world. But God called Joseph prosperous when he owned nothing, not even his own life! Biblical prosperity is the ability to use God's power and provision to meet our needs and the needs of others. The Bible calls Joseph a prosperous man even though, in the world's eyes, he was a mere slave. A man who is prosperous by the world's standards, but who is stingy and who lives independent of God, is not prosperous in the sight of God.

Joseph's master saw that the Lord was with Joseph. How wonderful it would be if the employers of all Christians could see that the Lord was with them. Imagine your

HOW TO MAKE YOUR GOD-GIVEN DREAM COME TRUE | 25

He gives you will be strong, such that you will just know that you know that you know that it is true! This is exactly what the Lord did for Joseph. He gave him big dreams, to bless him and to use him to bless multitudes. Today that is still God's purpose when He gives us dreams.

Satan wants to kill your dream

Soon Joseph's jealous brothers could stand him no longer. They took him and sold him into slavery, and eventually he ended up in the Egypt (Genesis 37:12-36). Just imagine the kind of frustration that led Joseph's brothers to almost kill him, and eventually sell him as a slave. The devil must have laughed at him and told him that now his dreams could never be fulfilled. It doesn't matter what you are going through today, or what your background may be. There is someone in the Bible who has experienced it, or even worse, and who came out victorious!

Don't use your mouth to delay your dream

When God reveals something to you, you need to be very careful when it comes to whom you share it with. Not everybody is going to be as excited as you are about what God has shown you; not even fellow Christians. You do not need to share everything that the Lord reveals to you with others. By doing so, you could get the enemy involved in God's plan for your life. Joseph found this out the hard way. He was only seventeen and didn't know better than to provoke his already jealous brothers with his dreams of rulership over them! Moses' mistake in this regard cost him forty years! How true do the words of Jesus in the book of Matthew chapter 7 ring:

Spirit intimately. He is the One who will show us things to come.

Jesus said the Holy Spirit would glorify Him by taking what is His – that is His Word, His revelation of the plans He has for us in this life – and then the Spirit will declare them to us. Wasn't it beneficial for Peter when Jesus told him in John 21:18, that he was going to preach the gospel until he was old? Not too long after that, in the book of Acts chapter 12, Peter was thrown in jail. Pending his imminent execution, he was soundly asleep, secure in the knowledge that he was too young to die! Jesus' revelation to him of things to come helped to guide the way Peter lived. Praise God that today, He is still in the business of showing us things to come!

The purpose of having a dream

Every Bible character who walked with God and did exploits for Him, had a dream, a hope, or a vision; something that pointed him or her to a better future. We as believers have the best days of our lives ahead of us, not behind us. When people refer to "the good old days", they imply that today and the days ahead can only be worse. In the world, people who cannot see any hope for the future often resort to substance abuse to numb the pain of the present reality. Or worse still, they commit suicide. Thank God that is not our portion as believers. In Christ, the best is always yet to come as we move from glory to glory!

The Lord may not show you everything that is ahead but He will surely let you know something that will take a hold of your heart – maybe through a dream or a vision, or simply through the reading the scriptures. The vision

And this time, the sun, the moon, and the eleven stars bowed down to me."

So he told it to his father and his brothers; and his father rebuked him and said to him, "What is this dream that you have dreamed? Shall your mother and I and your brothers indeed come to bow down to the earth before you?" And his brothers envied him, but his father kept the matter in mind.

Genesis 37:2-11

Has God given you a dream? Let us find out, from the life of Joseph, what we can do to cooperate with God in bringing whatever dream He has given us to fulfillment. However, we must first understand how God uses the Holy Spirit to birth dreams in us and show us things that are yet to happen.

The role of the Holy Spirit

Nevertheless I tell you the truth. It is to your advantage that I go away; for if I do not go away, the Helper will not come to you; but if I depart, I will send Him to you

However, when He, the Spirit of truth, has come, He will guide you into all truth; for He will not speak on His own authority, but whatever He hears He will speak; and He will tell you things to come.

He will glorify Me, for He will take of what is Mine and declare it to you."

John 16:7, 13-14

Just as Jesus was committed to doing the will of the Father, so is the Holy Spirit. He is not going to speak other than what the Father tells Him. Furthermore, Jesus tells us in this passage that God wants us to know "things to come". Why would He want to show us things to come? I believe that it is so that we can prepare for them, or in some cases, change things where necessary. God is not interested in hiding secrets. He wants to reveal them to us. That is why it is to our benefit to get to know the Holy

Chapter Two

HOW TO MAKE YOUR GOD-GIVEN DREAM COME TRUE

The passage you are about to read is about Joseph, and the power of a God-given dream:

...Joseph, being seventeen years old, was feeding the flock with his brothers. And the lad was with the sons of Bilhah and the sons of Zilpah, his father's wives; and Joseph brought a bad report of them to his father.
Now Israel loved Joseph more than all his children, because he was the son of his old age. Also he made him a tunic of many colours. But when his brothers saw that their father loved him more than all his brothers, they hated him and could not speak peaceably to him.
Now Joseph had a dream, and he told it to his brothers; and they hated him even more. So he said to them, "Please hear this dream which I have dreamed: There we were, binding sheaves in the field. Then behold, my sheaf arose and also stood upright; and indeed your sheaves stood all around and bowed down to my sheaf."
And his brothers said to him, "Shall you indeed reign over us? Or shall you indeed have have dominion over us?" So they hated him even more for his dreams and for his words. Then he dreamed still another dream and told it to his brothers, and said, "Look, I have dreamed another dream.

If you are ready to wake up, and ready to move on to that place of greater glory and greater blessing, then pray this prayer with all sincerity:

"Not my will Lord, but Your will be done. Anywhere you want me to go, I will go. I will do whatever You want me to do. I will live the way You want me to live. Father, I consecrate my life to You. I yield myself to You and depend on You and You alone. I refuse to sleep. I will stay alert and be sensitive to all that You are doing in this day and age. I will follow and fulfill Your plan for my life. In the Name of Jesus, Amen."

Now wake up, and get going!

of the Lord, and became a leader in the early church. The good news is that though we may fall, our faith need not fail. You might say that things turned out great for Peter and the others because Jesus prayed for them personally, but remember that Jesus is in you, and your prayers for yourself or for others, can be just as effective!

Before Jesus left the earth, He knew His report card. You too should know your report card before you leave. Determine where you are spiritually right now then start drawing closer to God by desiring the things of God more than you do the things of the world. Increase your spiritual hunger; desire to know God more. Do not allow natural things to take the place of spiritual things in your life. What you desire, and how much you desire it, is the thermometer to use to measure your spiritual temperature. Are you hot or are you cold?

Consecrate yourself to God. Tell Him that you are willing to yield your all to Him. Tell Him that you want His will to be done in your life, not yours. Ask God to take away anything that stands in His way. He won't just ask you for the sinful things in your life. He will also ask you for things that are not sinful in themselves, but which might hinder you in one way or another. He asked Abraham for the most precious thing in his life – his son Isaac. When Abraham gave Isaac to God, God gave Isaac back to him in the form of a whole nation!

to China! God just wanted to know that he was willing to go there, or anywhere else! Imagine all those years that he had wasted avoiding God, just because he was not willing.

It is important that we always keep a willing heart, and that we never let natural things and activities dull our sensitivity to the voice and direction of God. We must stay alert in the spirit.

Don't let your faith fail

And the Lord said, 'Simon, Simon! Indeed, Satan has asked for you, that he may sift you as wheat. But I have prayed for you, that your faith should not fail; and when you have returned to Me, strengthen your brethren.

Luke 22:31-32

God had a plan for Peter and Jesus knew that the devil also had plans for him. Satan had planned to 'sift' Peter as wheat. To 'sift' means 'to pulverize or break down closely by testing'. When Jesus had prayed ahead of time, He had prayed not only for Himself, but also for Peter and the other disciples. They had fled and Satan thought he had them, but Jesus had prayed them through. They were bound to come back like a boomerang! Jesus took His responsibility for His disciples seriously and that's why in His prayer in the book of John chapter 17 He said:

While I was with them in the world, I kept them in Your name. Those whom You gave Me I have kept; and none of them is lost except the son of perdition, that the Scripture might be fulfilled.

John 17:12

Peter had failed as a person, but because of what Jesus did for him, his faith did not fail. He repented of his denial remember what was done to you, but because you choose to act on the Word of God and forgive, the memories of the events will cease to be painful and damaging.

Joseph was fruitful in the land of his affliction, and you too can be fruitful in the land in which God has placed you. Joseph was able to let go of his past and let God bring his dreams to fulfillment. If you can do that too, you and all those around you will reap the benefits, now and eternally! No devil is big enough to steal your dream, and no sin should be enticing enough to cause you to abort it. Cooperate with the Holy Spirit, and together you will see the fulfillment of all the dreams that God has given you!

Chapter Three
GENERATIONAL CURSES: THE TRUTH REVEALED
(PART I)

People experience different problems in life. Some believe that their problems are the results of generational curses which run in their family. In this chapter and the next, we will determine whether or not a believer can be subject to the influence of a generational curse.

Abraham's blessings are ours

What did God promise Abraham? Blessings or curses? Blessings! Abraham was blessed to the point that anybody who came against him was cursed by God. In the book of Genesis chapter 12, God made a promise to Abraham saying:

> "I will make you a great nation; I will bless you and make your name great; and you shall be a blessing.
> I will bless those who bless you, and I will curse him who curses you; and in you all the families of the earth shall be blessed."
>
> *Genesis 12:2-3*

Galatians 3:29 tells us that *"if you are Christ's, then you are Abraham's seed, and heirs according to the promise"*. Praise God those same blessings of Abraham's are ours today!

In Exodus 20:6 and 34:7, God said that He would visit the iniquities of the fathers upon the children unto the third and fourth generation. But we cannot on the basis of these verses, conclude that we as believers are automatically subject to the effects of our forefathers' sins through generational curses.

Progressive revelation

The revelation of God in the Bible is progressive. That means that as you read from Genesis to the New Testament, you will find that more and more of God - His nature and His will - is being revealed to man. So David knew more about God than the people in Abraham's time, and the people who lived in the time of Hezekiah knew more about God and the things of God revealed to them than David did during his time. The people in the latter generations had what had been revealed in prior times along with the things that were revealed during their time. In the New Testament, those who were with Jesus knew more about God than the people in Hezekiah's time. The people who experienced Pentecost knew more about God than even those who saw Jesus in the flesh. And today, we in the church know much more about God than those before us, back in the days of Jesus.

Many of the false doctrines around resulted from picking something from the Old Testament which is not supported concretely by New Testament scripture. We do not develop doctrines from the Old Testament. Rather, church doctrines are developed from the New Testament, while the Old Testament is used to corroborate what the New Testament teaches. Never forget that we are living under the New Covenant, not the Old Covenant.

There is a devil out there who knows more about the Bible than many Christians do. You have to know the Bible so well that when the devil comes with his lies, you will be able to recognize his deception. That is what Jesus did when Satan came quoting scripture out of context in order to tempt Him. Jesus successfully resisted him with the Word of God.

Redeemed from every curse

How do people experience curses in their lives today? The same way they always have. In their bodies, with sickness and disease; in bad relationships and miserable lives; in poverty and lack; in premature death. If you read Deuteronomy 28:15-68 you will see an extensive list of every conceivable human curse. And just in case anything was left out in the list, verse 61 says, *"Also every sickness and every plague, which is not written in this Book of the Law, will the Lord bring upon you until you are destroyed."* Sin and disobedience to God will always bring a curse on us.

Thank God however, the book of Galatians chapter 3 tells us that Jesus became a curse for us. He became every evil that is in the world. Jesus has redeemed us from every curse, and that includes any generational curse!

> *Christ has redeemed us from the curse of the law, having become a curse for us (for it is written, 'Cursed is everyone who hangs on a tree'), that the blessing of Abraham might come upon the Gentiles (THAT'S US!) in Christ Jesus, that we might receive the promise of the Spirit through faith.*
>
> **Galatians 3:13-14**

An example of a generational curse could be alcoholism. Someone could claim that because their father and grandfather were alcoholics, and some of their siblings are alcoholics, then the curse of alcoholism runs in their family, and they can't help being an alcoholic too. The truth of the matter is that this is often a case of learned behaviour, which is learned consciously or otherwise.

The choice is yours

"Yet you say, 'Why should the son not bear the guilt of the father?' Because the son has done what is lawful and right, and has kept all My statutes and observed them, he shall surely live. The soul who sins shall die. The son shall not bear the guilt of the father, nor the father bear the guilt of the son. The righteousness of the righteous shall be upon himself, and the wickedness of the wicked shall be upon himself.

Ezekiel 18:19-20

Here God is saying that though previous generations have been evil, because their children have **chosen** to do good, they will have life. The sins of the father will no longer be visited on the children as had been stated back in Exodus. Remember that the Bible is progressive revelation.

The decision is yours, not your parents' or forefathers'. **Your choice for righteousness or wickedness will determine whether you experience a blessing or a curse in your life.** Choose to live by the Word of God, and His blessings will come to you. It doesn't matter what you have done, or how terrible you have been, Jesus can turn it around. There is more than enough grace to give you a fresh start. Your future will not have any semblance of your past or of any evil in your family.

Many people blame their circumstances in life on their parents. That is just their way of explaining their failures, and putting the blame on someone else. No matter how badly you were treated, or how evil the things your parents or ancestors dabbled into were, the choices you make today are what will determine what your future will be like. Once you are saved, the curses of those who came before you cannot come on you. Why? Because Jesus was made a curse for you, and He has redeemed you from EVERY curse! Alleluia!

Death in Adam, Life in Christ

Paul's writings in the book of Romans chapter 5 are a wonderful example of Biblical jurisprudence, from which we can learn that much of the teaching on generational curses is actually fallacious.

> *And not only that, but we also rejoice in God through our Lord Jesus Christ, through whom we have now received the reconciliation.*
>
> *Therefore, just as through one man sin entered the world, and death through sin, and thus death spread to all men, because all sinned (For until the law sin was in the world, but sin is not imputed when there is no law. Nevertheless death reigned from Adam to Moses, even over those who had not sinned according to the likeness of the transgression of Adam, who is a type of Him who was to come.*
>
> Romans 5:11-14

'Death' here is spiritual and signifies sin, sickness, disease, poverty, lack, - all the curses. Neither Adam nor Moses could stop death. The same way death reigned in them, it reigns over everyone, even those who have not transgressed a direct command. Even newborn babies had death reigning in them. Psalm 51:5 says that "...*I was brought forth in iniquity, and in sin my mother conceived me.*" Even in the womb, sin had taken hold. We didn't have to personally commit a sin - we were already in it because of Adam.

What did the baby who was born addicted to cocaine because of its mother's cocaine habit do to deserve such a condition? Nothing! In life, people often get what they do not deserve, suffering because of the sins of others. The truth is that we do not deserve what Jesus did for us either, but we can nevertheless take advantage of the benefits of His sacrifice.

The devil knew that if he could get Adam to sin, then he would get all mankind. Through Adam, all men were condemned. Now there is a new Adam! The Bible calls Him the second and last Adam. Adam was the progenitor, the father of a race of people called sinners. Now there is a new Father, of a different race of people called believers! That Father is Jesus.

Your family roots matter

But the free gift is not like the offense. For if by the one man's offense many died, much more the grace of God and the gift by the grace of the one Man, Jesus Christ, abounded to many. And the gift is not like that which came through the one who sinned. For the judgment which came from one offense resulted in condemnation, but the free gift which came from many offenses resulted in justification. For if by the one man's offense death reigned through the one, much more those who receive abundance of grace and of the gift of righteousness will reign in life through the One, Jesus Christ.)

Romans 5:15-17

We are now living in the time called the dispensation of grace; God is giving out grace to all men. That grace is more abundant than the sin or the death. The devil got Adam and condemned the whole human race. God sent Jesus as a man to come and undo all that Satan had done to mankind.

How did we all sin? Because of what one man, Adam, did. How were we made righteous? Because of what one man, Jesus, did. Do not put stock in your Adamic or natural, human heritage. **It doesn't matter who is in your family line, what they did, or who cursed them. As a believer, you now trace your roots back to Christ. Thank God His lineage is pure, nothing but blessings all the way through!** Adam was your father. Every human family goes all the way back to him. But now your family roots only go back to Christ, the Second Adam, and there are no curses in His family! Your trust and confidence as a believer should only be in your Christian heritage, not in who your earthly parents are.

Reigning through righteousness

There are curses out there. This whole atmosphere is infested with demonic power. If you as a Christian believe you can be subject to the influence of a generational curse, it will indeed affect you. When you start to claim what your great-grandfather, grandfather and father did, or what they had, and you believe you might have it too, then the devil will do his best to ensure that you start seeing signs to confirm that you do have it. For example, four generations of a family might have all died from the same disease. People would say that "it runs in the family". Each generation believes it, and the devil gets away with it.

If curses really do apply automatically, why then don't blessings fall on people automatically too? Shouldn't we be able to conclude just as easily that children from good families will turn out great, because "goodness runs in within the family"? Of course not, we all know of children from good families who have turned out horribly wrong.

Romans 5:17 says that to reign in life, to reign over sin, Satan and all his curses, we must receive abundance of grace and the free gift of righteousness from God through Jesus Christ. All our human righteousness is nothing but filthy rags (Isaiah 64:6). You can try to clean yourself up and make yourself pleasing to God, but you will not succeed. You will still be filthy before Him. We do not deserve this gift, neither can we earn it. We have to receive it by faith.

> *Therefore, as through one man's offense judgment came to all men, resulting in condemnation, even so through one Man's righteous act the free gift came to all men, resulting in justification of life.*
>
> *Romans 5:18*

Justification means that God sees us just as if we had never sinned! When Adam sinned, he lost consciousness of the righteousness, or right standing that he had with God.

> *For He made Him who knew no sin to be sin for us, that we might become the righteousness of God in Him.*
>
> *2 Corinthians 5:21*

Now that we are the righteousness of God in Christ, we can come into the presence of God, without guilt or condemnation. Were you involved in Adam's sin? No. Are you involved in the consequences of Adam's sin?

Yes. Were you involved in sending Jesus to come here to die? No. Can you partake of the benefits of His coming? Yes, yes, yes!

So if someone asks you today if you are righteous, the answer is an emphatic, "YES"! You have received a gift from God, you didn't work for it. Righteousness is not the same as holiness. Holiness has to do with your conduct, the quality of your life, what you do. Righteousness refers to who you are by virtue of your new birth, not what you do. You are born righteous, but you must live holy.

Exercise your authority
No matter who or what your parents were or did, thank God that Jesus is now the source of your lineage. Start believing that, and lay hold of your spiritual heritage, not your Adamic heritage. This in no way minimizes the terrible things people experience in life - for example, physical, mental or sexual abuse. But why should what somebody did to you mar you for the rest of your life?

"Confess your trespasses to one another, and pray for one another, that you may be healed. The effective, fervent prayer of a righteous man avails much.", James 5:16. Our prayers are going to be answered because of the righteousness that we have in Christ. The Amplified Bible renders this verse thus:

> *Confess to one another therefore your faults (your slips, your false steps, your offenses, your sins) and pray [also] for one another, that you may be healed and restored [to a spiritual tone of mind and heart]. The earnest (heartfelt, continued) prayer of a righteous man makes tremendous power available [dynamic in its working].*
>
> *James 5:16 (AMP)*

It is not the number of people who are praying that make the difference. Elijah for example, was only one man,. He prayed on the basis of the limited righteousness he had by the blood of a lamb. He was human just like us. He prayed earnestly for the rain to stop and sealed up the heavens for over three years. Then he prayed for the rain to come and it started to rain again (James 5:17-18).

How much more then can you and I, the righteousness of God in Christ, change the course of our lives, our families, and our world, by exercising our authority over the devil! Satan wants you to look at your natural heritage, your earthly family, rather than your spiritual heritage. He seeks to rob you of your righteousness consciousness, thereby robbing you of your ability to contact heaven and make changes down here on earth.

Generational curses are out there but no Christian should have to suffer the effects of any curse, generational or otherwise. If you believe they will affect you, they will. When someone tells you you need to be delivered from a generational curse and they pray over you, you might 'feel' delivered. But over time you might not be sure anymore, especially if you start seeing evidence of the curse again in your life. Next thing you know, you will be going for another 'deliverance session'.

Such a pattern only leads to bondage. The devil would have successfully robbed you of your righteousness consciousness. You won't be able to pray with confidence. Our prayers are answered because of Jesus' righteousness, not because of our family; not because we give money to the poor; not because we are good people.

What does it matter who your earthly father or ancestors are, when God is your heavenly Father? Christ has redeemed you from every curse, so by faith resist the devil and resist the effects of any curse you see trying to manifest in your life. Take full advantage of all your blessings in Christ, and no devil in hell will be big enough to stop you.

If you are not saved, you must first make Jesus your Saviour and Lord. Forsake the curses of your old Adamic family, then you can begin to enjoy the blessings of your new family in Christ!

Chapter Four
GENERATIONAL CURSES: THE TRUTH REVEALED
(PART II)

Some time ago, there was a Christian who held a university degree in agriculture. He decided to put into practice what he had learned and became a farmer. Neighboring fields all around his thrived, but in spite of his best efforts, his crops did not do well. His father had also been an unsuccessful farmer, as was his grandfather. His investigations soon revealed that for four generations his family had been unsuccessful in farming, all because of a curse that had been placed on them by an enemy.

He was advised that this generational curse had to be broken, and prayer was made to break the curse. He went back to farming and things started to pick up. However, three years later he was once again an unsuccessful farmer. So, he returned to the same people, to help him break the curse again. Could this child of God have handled the situation differently, in order to ensure permanent victory?

Your new family in Christ

> *Nevertheless death reigned from Adam to Moses, even over those who had not sinned according to the likeness of the transgression of Adam, who is a type of Him who was to come. But the free gift is not like the offense. For if by the one man's offense many died, much more the grace of God and the gift by the grace of the one Man, Jesus Christ, abounded to many.*
>
> *For if by the one man's offense death reigned through the one, much more those who receive abundance of grace and of the gift of righteousness will reign in life through the One, Jesus Christ.)*
>
> Romans 5:14-15, 17

When Adam and Eve sinned, a curse came on them and on us. You and I were in the Garden of Eden. How? We were in Adam's loins. The Bible says that all have sinned and fallen short of the glory of God. We did not have to lie, steal or kill to become a sinner. Sinner is who we were, for we were born in sin. Adam made that choice for us.

Adam was the father of a race of human beings, called sinners. Jesus is the progenitor, the father of a brand new race called saints, who are the righteousness of God. How do we become sinners? We are born that way. How do we become righteous? We have to be born that way, and that happens the moment we accept Jesus as Lord. Righteous is who you are. It is that unreserved ability, that unreserved right we have to come into the presence of God like we had never sinned, and to be treated by God the same way He would treat Jesus. Jesus earned that right for us, while Adam earned the right for us to become sinners.

"Death" in Romans 5:17 refers to any curse that brings about poverty, lack, sickness, disease, or death. Whether you call it a generational curse or the curse of the law, a curse is a curse. It is bad. You do not need to know what it is to realize that you do not want it!

Anything in your Adamic lineage, from you all the way back to Adam, is the result of the curse and of sin. Jesus took care of it by His blood and what He did for us on Calvary. Now that we belong to the family of God, by faith we can take advantage of our redemption in Christ, and we can effectively resist any curse.

There may have been people in your family who had a disease that killed them at a certain age. You are now at that age and the same symptoms are trying to come on you, telling you that you are going to die. What you need to do, is say "no" to those symptoms in the name of Jesus, and tell them to go back to the devil from whom they came in the first place! All of Adam's curses and anything that may have been passed down to you through your family (every family on earth can be traced back to Adam), can be stopped. Those of us who have received God's abundant grace and the gift of righteousness, shall reign in this life because of all that Jesus Christ has done for us! Alleluia!

Let us go back to the case of the farmer. He thought the curse was broken for three years, but as soon as the problems returned he conclude that the curse was back, and it had to be broken again. I believe his problem was that he did not realize just how persistent the devil is. He may depart for a season, but only to prepare to launch a counter attack. What the farmer needed to have done, was to stand his ground and resist the devil, and then he would have had no choice but to flee. (1 Peter 5:8-9, Luke 4:1-13.)

The farmer did not need any generational curses broken. Jesus became the embodiment of all curses. The book of 2 Corinthians chapter 5 tells us;

> *Therefore, if anyone is in Christ, he is a new creation; old things have passed away; behold, all things have become new.*
>
> 2 Corinthians 5:17

The next verse affirms that these 'new' then are of God. We as Believers are not living under any curses. But if you believe you are, you then submit yourself under the devil's whims and caprices. The devil will play games with you while holding you captive at his will.

Better covenant, better promises

> *The soul who sins shall die. The son shall not bear the guilt of the father, nor the father bear the guilt of the son. The righteousness of the righteous shall be upon himself, and the wickedness of the wicked shall be upon himself.*
> *But if a wicked man turns from all his sins which he has committed, keeps all My statutes, and does what is lawful and right, he shall surely live; he shall not die.*
>
> Ezekiel 18:20-21

Moses had said that God would visit the iniquity of the fathers upon their children, up to the third and fourth generation. That was the case in Israel until the time of Ezekiel the prophet. Now, God was telling Israel that from the time of Ezekiel's prophecy forward, the soul who sins is the one who will die. The sons will no longer have to suffer for the sins of their fathers. The sinner who turns to God in repentance, will have the curses stayed in his life.

If this was true back under the old covenant, then what about now that we live under a new covenant based upon better promises; shouldn't we be even more confident? Confident that once we are saved, all the works of Satan and the effects of our sin (or any ancestor's sin) have been permanently stopped by faith in Jesus.

Know and exercise your covenant rights

> *Now He was teaching in one of the synagogues on the Sabbath. And behold, there was a woman who had a spirit of infirmity eighteen years, and was bent over and could in no way raise herself up. But when Jesus saw her, He called her to Him and said to her, "Woman, you are loosed from your infirmity."*
>
> *Luke 13:10-12*

This can apply to us. Today, Jesus by His Spirit is still calling people to Himself to bless them. He didn't call this woman to Himself to multiply her sorrows. So why should your becoming a Christian today multiply or intensify the work of the enemy in your life? Jesus didn't bother to find out if this was a generational curse or not. All He cared about was that she was a child of Abraham, and she had a covenant with God, which included healing. Thus she had a right to be free from her bondage.

> *And He laid His hands on her, and immediately she was made straight, and glorified God.*
>
> *Luke 13:13*

Notice that though Jesus did not cast out the spirit, the spirit obviously left. He just spoke in faith and the devil could not stay! **Do you know that the devil is actually scared of you? He is so scared that he hopes and prays (not to God!) that you will never realize what God has done for you in Christ. For he knows that the day you realize it, will be the day he can no longer terrorize you.** Once you know the truth, it will set you free!

> But the ruler of the synagogue answered with indignation, because Jesus had healed on the Sabbath; and he said to the crowd, "There are six days on which men ought to work; therefore come and be healed on them, and not on the Sabbath day."
>
> Luke 13:14

Do you know why Jesus healed so many people on the Sabbath? "Sabbath" means rest. That is the name of the dispensation we are living in now - the dispensation of grace, the dispensation of rest. Canaan's land was a land of rest, blessing and increase. Jesus' healing on the Sabbath signified that this new dispensation was going to be a dispensation of the blessings and grace of God. (See the book of Hebrews chapters 3 and 4)

> The Lord then answered him and said, "Hypocrite![a] Does not each one of you on the Sabbath loose his ox or donkey from the stall, and lead it away to water it? ^{16} So ought not this woman, being a daughter of Abraham, whom Satan has bound—think of it—for eighteen years, be loosed from this bond on the Sabbath?"
>
> Luke 13:15-16

False religion always lifts animals above people. Healing and ministering to the physical body, to this ruler, was a carnal thing - simply not good enough to take place on the Sabbath day. Jesus had to change that kind of thinking. He couldn't care less if it was the Sabbath day or not. This woman, as a child of Abraham, should not have been bound in the first place. She lived with the curse for eighteen years, not knowing that she could have been free from it. If she had not met Jesus, she probably would have been bound for another eighteen or more years.

These so-called generational curses have perpetrated themselves in the lives of Christians because of their ignorance of the word of God; ignorance of their covenant rights. We should not be going from one place to another seeking those who we think can break the power of generational curses over us. In Christ we have no curse to our name. What people call generational curses are actually curses already included in the curse of the law. *(See Deuteronomy 28:14-68).*

> *Christ has redeemed us from the curse of the law, having become a curse for us (for it is written, 'Cursed is everyone who hangs on a tree'), that the blessings of Abraham might come upon the Gentiles (US) in Christ Jesus, that we might receive the promise of the Spirit through faith.*
>
> *Galatians 3:13-14*

You must wake up to the fact that no generational curses in your family should affect you. Realize that when you said "YES" to Jesus, it meant "NO" to the devil, and "NO" to all his works in your life. The farmer we spoke of earlier should have woken up to that fact. No special service was needed to set him free. He could have been free in the same way that Jesus set that woman free.

Who sinned?

> *Now as Jesus passed by, He saw a man who was blind from birth. And His disciples asked Him, saying, "Rabbi, who sinned, this man or his parents, that he was born blind?"*
> *Jesus answered, "Neither this man nor his parents sinned, but that the works of God should be revealed in him.*
>
> *John 9:1-3*

The disciples wanted to know if the man's blindness was the result of his sin, or the sin of someone else in his family. In short, they were asking if it could be the result of a generational curse? Jesus replied that it is possible for people to experience curses that have nothing to do with their past, or what their ancestors did. The devil however, can lie to you and say that things are going wrong in your life because of what your great grandfather did. Once you believe that, you open the door for him to come and work in your life.

John 9:3(b), *"...but that the works of God should be revealed in him."* Is Jesus then saying that God created this man blind so that when He came to the earth He could get him healed and thereby be glorified? What a cheap way that would be for God to get glory! This man could have been blind for the same reason that the woman in Luke 13 was crippled. The fact that neither he nor his parents, knew their rights as the seed of Abraham to have fullness of health.

He did not deserve his blindness, he had not sinned as a baby and it had nothing to do with his parents even though they were not sinless. Some religious people might say that since God knows everything, He knew this man would do something terrible later in life, so God gave him his punishment ahead of time! Most times religion can be so nasty in its reasoning, always judging God as the villain. No wonder people don't want to know a God like that!

Take a look at the book of John chapter 9:

> *"I must work the works of Him who sent Me while it is day; the night is coming when no one can work. As long as I am in the world, I am the light of the world."*
>
> *John 9:4-5*

By healing this man, Jesus was saying that this seed of Abraham had the right to be free. **He was full of eager yearning to set the bound and the oppressed free. It made no difference to Jesus how the curses came on them in the first place.** Acts 10:38 says that:

...God anointed Jesus of Nazareth with the Holy Spirit and with power, who went about doing good and healing all who were oppressed by the devil, for God was with Him."

Acts 10:38

If Jesus set that man free, today He will do the same for you and me. For Hebrews 13:8 states that Jesus Christ is "the same yesterday, today, and forever."

No automatic blessings

Unfortunately, many Christians believe so much in the power of generational curses that they seem to have more confidence in them than they have in Jesus! Their faith in Satan is his license to hold them in bondage. You have to check your belief system. What do you believe? If light is stronger than darkness, love is stronger that hate, then blessings should be stronger than curses. If God is stronger than Satan, then why don't people talk about "generational blessings"? For example, if a man who is the son and grandson of faithful Christians is living a godless, sinful lifestyle, why don't people say this of him: "Oh, don't worry about him, he'll turn out alright. Generational blessings are going to catch up with him, regardless of how he's living." No! In order to enjoy God's blessings, he must personally fulfill the conditions in God's word.

Blessings are not in your genes. You do not impart them biologically to your children. We teach our children the word of God, by our words and by our actions. That is how the blessings will be carried on in a family. When parents read their Bibles, speak the word and live by God's principles, their children learn to do so too. If the parents get drunk and fight a lot, then the children will learn the same behaviour – that is simply learned behaviour, not a generational curse as some would like to call it.

Throughout the book of Deuteronomy, God instructed Israel to study His word, understand it, practice it and teach it, then they would have a prosperous life.

> *Every commandment which I command you today you must be careful to observe that you may live and multiply, and go in and possess the land of which the Lord swore to your fathers.*
>
> *Deuteronomy 8:1*

They had to do something in order to experience the blessings of God. The blessings would not come automatically just because they were the seed of Abraham.

That promised land of Canaan represented all the blessings that you and I want to receive today – healing; prosperity; a peaceful, loving home; children who are serving the Lord; etc. Nothing was guaranteed to them just because they were God's covenant people. Neither is anything guaranteed to you today, just because you are saved.

Paul prayed in Ephesians 1:18 that *"the eyes of your understanding* (the eyes of your heart) *being enlightened; that you may know what is the hope of His calling, what are the riches of the glory of His inheritance in the saints."* God wants us to realize how rich we are in Christ, and that everything we need is already provided for us in Him.

Some Christians have the mindset that they do not have what they need to obtain and keep the victory. So they erroneously go around seeking some 'spiritual' person to lay hands on them, and give it to them. (No doubt there is a valid ministry of laying on of hands.)

You will find it most beneficial to pray the prayers in Ephesians 1:17-23 and 3:14-19 over yourself everyday. Personalize them and pray like this:

"I pray that the God of our Lord Jesus Christ, the Father of glory, may give to me the spirit of wisdom and revelation in the knowledge of Him, the eyes of my understanding being enlightened; that I may know what is the hope of His calling, what are the riches of the glory of His inheritance in the saints...."

Purpose to become rock solid in the word of God so that when any of these wrong doctrines come around, you will recognize immediately that they are unscriptural. The Spirit of God inside you will tell you. Abraham's blessings are yours today and always. Believe it, receive it, and daily walk in it!

Chapter Five

WHEN THINGS GO FROM BAD TO WORSE

When things go from bad to worse, it is God's will for them to turn around to His glory and for our blessing. Indeed the Word of God has the answer to everything that we could possibly face. Once we learn how to make contact with God, we can always get what He desires for us and put the devil where he belongs. But how exactly do we receive from God? People often say that God can do anything He wants to do, whenever He wants to do it - and there is some truth to that. However, we do not necessarily receive from God on the basis of what He *can* do.

God's ability or your faith

In the book of Mark chapter 9, a desperate father brought his demon possessed boy to Jesus for help. The father begged Him;

> ...But if You can do anything, have compassion on us and help us."
> jesus said to him, "If you can believe, all things are possible to him who believes."
>
> *Mark 9: 22-23*

Notice how Jesus immediately put the responsibility back on the father; the question deciding the issue was not Jesus' power, but the man's faith.

Today people are still approaching God in the same way, "God, if You can, You do something for me." It is not so much what God can do, but what YOU can believe. Of the many miracles and healings that Jesus did during His earthly ministry, the Bible records only about 19 individual cases of healing. In at least 10 of those cases, the individual's faith is referred to as a key factor in their receiving their healing, and in some of the other cases it is implied. What can YOU comfortably believe God for? That is the deciding factor in YOUR receiving from God.

With this in mind, let us look at the story of Jairus and his sick daughter in the book of Mark chapter 5:21-43, where we can learn what to do when a bad situation gets even worse.

> *And behold, one of the rulers of the synagogue came, Jairus by name. And when he saw Him, he fell at His feet and begged Him earnestly, saying, "My little daughter lies at the point of death. Come and lay Your hands on her, that she may be healed, and she will live." So Jesus went with him, and a great multitude followed Him and thronged Him. (or pressed in on Him)*
>
> *Mark 5:22-24*

Jairus worshipped Jesus and got His attention. Whenever you see someone in the Bible do something that enabled them to receive from God, if you do the same thing, you will get the same results, for God is no respecter of persons. Your heartfelt worship will always get God's attention. Jairus did not ask Jesus to come and try and see what He could do. He knew what Jesus could do; he had heard about His healing ministry. So he said to Jesus,

"Come and lay Your hands on her ...and she shall live." He did not say, *"Come try it"*, or *"If it is Your will."* He knew for a certainty that she would live, and Jesus went with him.

Reading through the four gospel accounts, you will often find that the faith of an individual would cause Jesus to change from the direction in which He was headed, and follow them. Jesus did not go with Jairus because He liked the way he looked or because he had a lot of money. No. It was because of his faith. Remember, Jesus was going somewhere else when Jairus came up to Him and asked Him to go with him.

Obstacles in the way of faith

> *Now a certain woman had a flow of blood for twelve years, and had suffered many things from many physicians. She had spent all that she had and was no better, but rather grew worse. ²⁷ When she heard about Jesus, she came behind Him in the crowd and touched His garment. For she said, "If only I may touch His clothes, I shall be made well."*
>
> Mark 5:25-28

What had she heard? This Man had been anointed with the Holy Spirit and power and was going about doing good, healing people. Miracles were happening all around Jesus and He had brought untold joy to multitudes. So, when this woman heard about Jesus, she didn't just dismiss Him and put Him in the same class with all those physicians who had taken her money. It would have been easy to do that, considering the bad experience she had had with the others. But if she had done that, we wouldn't be reading about her now.

In Bible times, such a woman was classified as unclean according to the book of Leviticus - not just hygienically, but also in a religious sense. No matter how rich you were, the moment you were declared unclean you would no longer be allowed to interact with normal people. This was probably a woman of great means who had lost all her wealth in treating her condition. So she had heard about Jesus, and was pushing her way through the crowd to reach Him. This woman had every reason in the world not to attempt to get close to Jesus. She was weak from hemorrhaging for twelve years; that crowd could crush her. She would have had to get rid of the garment she was required to wear as an unclean person, and disguise herself, hoping nobody would recognize her as she tried to touch Jesus.

Even if she did make it to Jesus, Jairus was standing with Him - the very person who had the authority under the religious order to have her stoned. In other words, this big obstacle was standing right next to her answer! She could have prayed for God to send him away, but Jairus wasn't about to leave till he got what he came for!

Some Christians are praying today for God to take away the obstacles in their lives. Such prayers are prayers of unbelief. This woman had serious obstacles that she had to overcome to get to Jesus. She was literally taking her life in her hands. To the ordinary eye she was taking a big risk, but for the person in faith it is no risk at all, only a wonderful leap of faith into victory!

Notice she said, *"If only I may touch His clothes, I SHALL be made well"* **Jesus needs your faith to help you.** You may have stumbling blocks, but they are supposed to be turned into stepping stones to your victory in Christ!

Immediately the fountain of her blood was dried up, and she felt in her body that she was healed of the affliction.

> *And Jesus, immediately knowing in Himself that power had gone out of Him, turned around in the crowd and said, "Who touched My clothes?"*
> *But His disciples said to Him, "You see the multitude thronging You, and You say, 'Who touched Me?'"*

Mark 5:29-31

Healing is not a feeling, but it will produce a feeling. She made contact with Jesus and the anointing from Him flowed into her body producing a healing and a cure. Immediately Jesus knew power had left Him. As far as the disciples were concerned, Jesus shouldn't have been asking who touched Him, but rather who *hadn't* touched Him! But Jesus wasn't talking about just any kind of touch. Not the touch of the curious who wanted to feel His skin or His clothes. The only touch the Master was aware of was the touch of faith. That should reveal to us that the Master is aware of every touch of faith. Smith Wigglesworth used to say that God will pass over a thousand people to get to one person with faith. It is that touch of faith that zapped the power out of Jesus without Him even knowing about her need. This woman wasn't wondering *if* it was God's will to heal her, or *if* she should be breaking the religious law. God is in a hurry to bless us, and He is not legalistic about it either.

Delay does not mean denial

> *And He looked around to see her who had done this thing. But the woman, fearing and trembling, knowing what had happened to her, came and fell down before Him and told Him the whole truth. And He said to her, "Daughter, your faith has made you well. Go in peace, and be healed of your affliction."*

Mark 5:32-34.

All this delay was probably making Jairus anxious about his daughter. But here was Jesus, giving this woman all the time she needed. Why? Because her story was a testimony of faith. He wanted the people to hear it, and to learn how to tap into the power of God! There was nothing Satan could do to Jairus' daughter (or that he can do to you), that God could not undo or reverse. **God is never late!**

Notice too that, though it was the power in Jesus that effected the healing, Jesus did not put the emphasis on His power, but on the woman's faith - *"Daughter your faith has made you well."* He was there with all the power, but the whole crowd wasn't getting healed. One woman's faith however, initiated the release of that healing power for her own benefit.

Don't be afraid, only believe

While He was still speaking, some came from the ruler of the synagogue's house who said, 'Your daughter is dead. Why trouble the Teacher any further?' As soon as Jesus heard the word that was spoken, He said to the ruler of the synagogue, 'do not be afraid, only believe.'

Mark 5:35-36

Jairus' bad situation had just gotten worse, his daughter was dead. The words that Jesus spoke to him are still the key to victory today; "Do not be afraid, only believe!"

Jesus did not stop to have a prayer meeting, make a few strong scripture confessions, or call a three day fast. Prayer is necessary, making confessions and fasting are good, but regardless of how much you pray, confess and fast, you are still going to have to obey this - *do not be afraid, only believe.* You can do every religious thing you know to do, but if you do not do this, you are NOT going to receive what God has in store for you.

Jesus needed Jairus' faith to help Him. If it were only dependent upon Jesus, He would have told Jairus not to bother about it, and that He would take care of the situation Himself. Remember, Jairus had said in verse 23, *"Come and lay Your hands on her, that she may be healed, and she will live."* - the only reason why Jesus had set out for Jairus' house in the first place was because of the faith he had expressed in Him.

Verse 37 reveals a key point, a place where many people lose their victory; *"And He permitted no one to follow Him except Peter, James and John..."*. No one was allowed to follow them. Jesus got rid of all the curiosity seekers, unbelieving friends, comforters, religious bigots and whoever else. You need people of like precious faith when the going gets tough.

When persecution arose against the early church and the apostles were released from detention in Acts chapter 4, they went to their own company. It is during difficult times that you need to come to church the most, not stay home and pray by yourself. You NEED your own company. Christians who do not belong to a church are open game to the devil. They are unbalanced, and are susceptible to false doctrines. When you are facing the heat of the trial, cut off all the things of the flesh; turn off those mindless TV programs!

Because He knew they believed like He did, Jesus only took Peter, James and John along with Him and Jairus. Don't go distributing your prayer requests to people who do not know how to pray. You need believers who can hold up with you, firm and strong. Not the kind who, when asked to pray for a deathly sick person, will pray, "Oh God, remember the sick and heal them if it be Your will. But if not, then we know You need another voice in the heavenly choir, so they are better off up there with You."

> Then He came to the house of the ruler of the synagogue, and saw a tumult and those who wept and wailed loudly. When He came in, He said to them, "Why make this commotion and weep? The child is not dead, but sleeping."
> And they ridiculed Him. But when He had put them all outside, He took the father and the mother of the child, and those who were with Him, and entered where the child was lying. Then He took the child by the hand, and said to her, "Talitha, cumi," which is translated, "Little girl, I say to you, arise." Immediately the girl arose and walked, for she was twelve years of age. And they were overcome with great amazement.
>
> Mark 5:38-42

Jesus put out all the unbelieving relatives and mourners, and that is what you need to do too. Put away from you all those who are not in faith, anyone and anything that is full of fear and unbelief. It may not be the nice thing to do, but because of what is at stake - someone else's life, it definitely is the right thing to do. Would you want to act nice to someone at the expense of your child's life? Jesus wasn't worried about being nice, and neither should you!

Jesus needs your faith

What had Jairus asked? He wanted Jesus to come and lay His hands on his daughter. What did Jesus do? He came and took the child by the hand and ministered to her. JESUS NEEDS YOUR FAITH TO HELP YOU. The devil would love to separate you from your faith. He will tell you that your faith is not strong enough. However, the very reason why he told you that is because your faith IS strong enough! You wouldn't expect the devil to come and tell you that you can believe God, and that all things are possible to you when you believe? No, he won't tell you that, for he lies all the time.

The greatest miracle that could ever take place is for a person to be born again. If you are saved, then the greatest thing that could happen to anybody has already happened to you. Every other thing in life is not as significant. So , whenever you face difficulties, and the devil starts lying to you that your faith is not strong enough, you just need to tell him, "*I am saved, filled with the Holy Spirit, and greater is He that is in me than he that is in the world. The Holy Ghost in me will put me over, you hide and watch devil, and there's nothing you can do to stop it!*" Alleluia! And so it will happen.

Jesus said, "*Do not be afraid, only believe.*" If you are afraid, you *cannot* believe - one excludes the other. In the book of John chapter 14, Jesus said...

> "*Let not your heart be troubled; you believe in God, believe also in Me.*"
>
> *John 14:1*

If your heart is troubled, you *cannot* believe in God. If you are believing God, then your heart will not be troubled. There are times when anxiety and fear will come against you. Your knees may be knocking from fear, but speak these words out of your mouth in faith, "*In the name of Jesus, I will not be afraid, I believe God and He is putting me over.*" Words like these come from your heart, your spirit. Your body is simply where your spirit lives, so it doesn't matter if your knees are knocking or not. You may feel the hot breath of the devil right on the back of your neck, but if you speak out words of faith you will always get the victory! All the enemy's lies and pressure are simply designed to get you to stop believing God.

Sometimes Christians mistakenly set a time limit when they are believing God for something. You may be believing God for a certain thing, and think that if it doesn't happen by say 3 o'clock on April the 30th, then you have a right to stop believing God for it. Why should a man-made device like a clock, be what tells you when to stop believing God? We are believers by nature, God made us that way. There is never a right time to stop believing God; there is never a right time to doubt. You won't know how strong your faith is until you use it, or step out on it.

You know where you are, what you are believing God for, and God knows where you are. No matter how bad things may seem, let faith arise in your heart today as you have heard the words of Jesus Himself, "**Do not be afraid, only believe!**"

Chapter Six
TOPPLING THE GIANTS IN YOUR LIFE

This might be news to you, but Satan does not like you one bit, especially if you have given your life to Christ and are a child of God. We all have an enemy to contend with, and his name is Satan, the enemy of our souls. He raises up enemies to attack us. Enemies like sickness and disease, poverty, family problems, and every other kind of a problem. Anywhere you have people, you have problems; people and problems go hand in hand. The truth of the matter is that as soon as you solve one problem, another one presents itself. Oftentimes, these problems seem like giants before us - intimidating, overwhelming, and seemingly undefeatable. God's word however, assures us of victory every time! So, let us take a look at some biblical steps required to bring down the giants in our lives.

A giant slayer of old
If ever there was a giant slayer, it was David. We find his story inthe book of 1 Samuel chapter 17. From this story we discover the secret to David's success in felling the

giant called Goliath. The Philistines were long-standing enemies of Israel and they had come out to fight Israel again. This time however, their champion Goliath came forward with a proposal.

> And a champion went out from the camp of the Philistines, named Goliath, from Gath whose height was six cubits and a span (nine feet nine inches). He had a bronze helmet on his head, and he was armed with a coat of mail, and the weight of the coat was five thousand shekels of bronze (one hundred and twenty six pounds). And he had bronze armor on his legs and a bronze javelin between his shoulders. Now the staff of his spear was like a weaver's beam, and his iron spear-head weighed six hundred shekels (about fifteen pounds); and a shield-bearer went before him. Then he stood and cried out to the armies of Israel, and said to them, 'Why have you come out to line up for battle? Am I not a Philistine, and you the servants of Saul? Choose a man for yourselves, and let him come down to me. If he is able to fight with me and kill me, then we will be your servants. But if I prevail against him and kill him, then you shall be our servants and serve us.' And the Philistine said, 'I defy the armies of Israel this day; give me a man, that we may fight together.' When Saul and all Israel heard these words of the Philistine, they were dismayed and greatly afraid.
>
> *I Samuel 17: 4-11*

Goliath came out to represent his country, and he wanted Israel to choose their best fighter to come and fight against him. The people of the loser would then have to serve the victor's people. For the Philistines to have come up with a proposition like this meant they knew they had the biggest soldier around. Even King Saul, the tallest of all of the Israelites, was not about to face him. He was just as scared as the rest of his men.

Today, Goliath would represent any type of monstrous problem that you may be facing. Perhaps you woke up this morning to a problem that you have never faced before in your life. Take comfort in that the Bible tells us that we are more than conquerors through Christ Jesus. Did you know that God expects you to win every battle you face? Not, win some, lose a few, but win every single battle. Failures are man-made, not God made, for God never fails. After he became king of Israel, David fought more wars than all the other kings of Israel put together and never lost a single one. The Bible tells us we have a better covenant today than what he had, and that our covenant is based on better promises. That's why we should do even better than David did.

Have faith in the covenant

> *Then as he talked with them, there was the champion, the Philistine of Gath, Goliath by name, coming up from the armies of the Philistines; and he spoke according to the same words. So David heard them. And all the men of Israel, when they saw the man, fled from him and were dreadfully afraid. So the men of Israel said, "Have you seen this man who has come up? Surely he has come up to defy Israel; and it shall be that the man who kills him the king will enrich with great riches, will give him his daughter, and give his father's house exemption from taxes in Israel."*
> *Then David spoke to the men who stood by him, saying, "What shall be done for the man who kills this Philistine and takes away the reproach from Israel? For who is this uncircumcised Philistine, that he should defy the armies of the living God?"*
>
> I Samuel 17:23-27

David arrived on the scene and heard the same words that Israel's army had been hearing for the last 40 days, but his response was different. Instead of getting scared, he got bold and mad and was ready to go and face the giant. "What audacity, to challenge the armies of the living God, who does he think he is?!", David thought. Israel's trained soldiers, veterans, were all paralyzed with fear, but David, a boy not even old enough to serve in the army, rose up in faith and righteous indignation! How was that possible? We get a clue to the answer from the way David referred to Goliath; "*Who is this **uncircumcised** Philistine?*" By this statement, David was saying I have a covenant with God through circumcision, but Goliath doesn't. I have God on my side, he doesn't. Therefore he is no match for me and my God!

In the book of Genesis chapter 17 we read how God cut a covenant with Abraham, and through him, with all his descendants, the Israelites.

> *And God said to Abraham: "As for you, you shall keep My covenant, you and your descendants after you throughout their generations. This is My covenant which you shall keep, between Me and you and your descendants after you: Every male child among you shall be circumcised; and you shall be circumcised in the flesh of your foreskins, and it shall be a sign of the covenant between Me and you.*
>
> *Genesis 17:9-11*

The covenant was cut by circumcision. But, what was this covenant? It was a divine, super strong agreement between God and Israel. The covenant brought blessings when complied with, and curses when it was broken.

The book of Deuteronomy is essentially one long exhortation from Moses to the children of Israel as he prepared them to enter Canaan, the Promised Land. In it, Moses writes in detail about the covenant and how they were supposed to walk with God. In chapter 28 we read:

> *"The Lord will cause your enemies who rise against you to be defeated before your face; they shall come out against you one way and flee before you seven ways."*
>
> *Deuteronomy 28:7*

Here God is simply saying that your winning does not depend on your ability or skill. **He** will deliver your enemies into your hands! "They shall come against you one way, and flee from you seven ways." That seems to imply that you are invincible and you are guaranteed victory as long as you walk in the covenant.

David knew the word of God and believed it and that is why he was so taken aback by everyone else's fearful reaction to Goliath. He was probably thinking, *"Are they in their right minds? Don't they know the covenant? God has already told us that our enemies will flee from us. And to top it all, I can't believe that King Saul is going to lavish such riches on someone just for killing this guy!"*

Even though David had no battle experience, notice that he did not stop to pray about whether or not to take up Goliath's challenge. We do not need to pray about what the Bible already tells us belongs to us, or tells us we should do. For instance, the Bible says that we should tithe. We do not need to pray about whether or not we should tithe; we just need to do it. The word of God says we should not forsake the assembling of ourselves together. We do not need to pray about it, we just need to do it.

A comparable situation to David's would be where a person receives a bad report from their doctor. They have just found out that they have a terminal illness and have only a short time left to live. Most people would simply collapse at such news. Fear would cause them to die many times before death even strikes! Some other people however, on hearing the same report, would respond in faith and get mad at the devil - *"How dare you put this on me Satan! I don't have time to be sick. Devil, you won't try this on me again. I will definitely be healed in the name of the Lord Jesus Christ!"*

You need revelation knowledge
Throughout history we can see how ordinary people have accomplished extraordinary feats. They were able to do these great works because they had a revelation that others did not have. Albert Einstein and Thomas Edison were such men. Electricity was here on earth even in the Garden of Eden, but it wasn't until someone came along thousands of years later, that we knew how to harness it and make use of it. Likewise, if you are ever going to do anything for God you will have to have a revelation of who He is and who you are in Him. David knew he served a great God, and he knew that because of his covenant relationship with God, even the impossible was possible for him. How much more should we know that today?

That is why Paul, by the Holy Spirit, prayed in the book of Ephesians chapter 1:

> ...that the God of our Lord Jesus Christ, the Father of glory, may give to you the spirit of wisdom and revelation in the knowledge of Him, the eyes of your understanding[a] being enlightened; that you may know what is the hope of His calling, what are the riches of the glory of His inheritance in the saints, and what is the exceeding greatness of His power toward us who believe, according to the working of His mighty power...
>
> *Ephesians 1:17-19*

Pray this prayer over yourself daily and you will see results in your life.

Four steps to toppling a giant
When you read the book of 1 Samuel chapter 17 you will find the four steps that David used to bring down Goliath. From verses 26 to 47, he repeatedly stated what he was

going to do to the giant. The first step then, in felling your giant is to say it - that is, say that you are going to defeat it.

1. **SAY IT**

   > Then David spoke to the men who stood by him, saying, "What shall be done for the man who kills this Philistine and takes away the reproach from Israel? For who is this uncircumcised Philistine, that he should defy the armies of the living God?"
   > Now Eliab his oldest brother heard when he spoke to the men; and Eliab's anger was aroused against David, and he said, "Why did you come down here? And with whom have you left those few sheep in the wilderness? I know your pride and the insolence of your heart, for you have come down to see the battle."
   > And David said, "What have I done now? Is there not a cause?" [30] Then he turned from him toward another and said the same thing; and these people answered him as the first ones did.
   > Now when the words which David spoke were heard, they reported them to Saul; and he sent for him. Then David said to Saul, "Let no man's heart fail because of him; your servant will go and fight with this Philistine."
   > Your servant has killed both lion and bear; and this uncircumcised Philistine will be like one of them, seeing he has defied the armies of the living God." Moreover David said, "The Lord, who delivered me from the paw of the lion and from the paw of the bear, He will deliver me from the hand of this Philistine."
   > And Saul said to David, "Go, and the Lord be with you!"
   >
   > 1 Samuel 17:26, 28-32, 36-37

The first thing you need to do to bring down the giants in your life is to **say it**. The Bible says that you can have what you say. Some people, even Christians, will get mad at you for making your boast in God and declaring what God will do for you - just like Eliab got mad at David. Declaring what God will do for you may have a semblance of pride to some, but in truth it is humility. You are only saying, *"I can't do it, but God can do it for me and I am willing to be a vessel."*

Every time you step up to do something for God, you are going to face challengers. So, do exactly what David did and detach yourself from such people. Make sure you declare what you are believing God for every time you have an opportunity to. When people come against you for saying it, just keep on saying it!

> So the Philistine came, and began drawing near to David, and the man who bore the shield went before him. And when the Philistine looked about and saw David, he disdained him; for he was only a youth, ruddy and good-looking. So the Philistine said to David, "Am I a dog, that you come to me with sticks?" And the Philistine cursed David by his gods. Then David said to the Philistine, "You come to me with a sword, with a spear, and with a javelin. But I come to you in the name of the Lord of hosts, the God of the armies of Israel, whom you have defied.
>
> 1 Samuel 17:41-43, 45

Do you know that the giants in your life will speak to you? Problems will talk to you. Depending on what your situation is, you might hear these words over and over again, "You are going to die. You are going to lose your family. You are going to fail. You are going bankrupt." You cannot stop the giants from talking to you, but as soon as they get through talking, make sure you say something back to them! Amen! Don't just keep quiet, open your mouth and speak the word of God in the name of Jesus: *"By the stripes of Jesus I was healed. I will live and not die, and declare the works of God in my life!"*

2. DO IT

The next step David took in felling his giant was that he **did it**. He did what he said he would do. What would it have been like if the appointed day of battle with Goliath came, and David failed to show up? Obviously then he would have been nothing more than a guy full of hot air with no substance. It is easy to talk big, but what is really important is to live up to your words. All David had to do was show up that day and the great God he had bragged about would be obliged to show Himself strong on David's behalf.

Nowadays too many Christians fail to keep their word. Their words are of no value. When they say something, they often do not do it. When you tell someone you are going to meet them at 6 p.m., make sure you are there at 6 p.m. When you tell someone you will do something for them, make sure you do it.

As you keep speaking words of faith like David did, the very thing you need to do will come up in your heart. Even when you do not see a way, God will make the way for you to do it. How did David know the weapon he needed to use against the giant? Saul tried to make the decision for him and offered David his armor; but it just did not feel right. Instead, David used the name of the Lord, and his sling and some stones - trusty weapons that he had proved over and over again.

> *This day the Lord will deliver you into my hand, and I will strike you and take your head from you. And this day I will give the carcasses of the camp of the Philistines to the birds of the air and the wild beasts of the earth, that all the earth may know that there is a God in Israel. Then all this assembly shall know that the Lord does not save with sword and spear; for the battle is the Lord's, and He will give you into our hands."*
> *So it was, when the Philistine arose and came and drew near to meet David, that David hurried and ran toward the army to meet the Philistine. Then David put his hand in his bag and took out a stone; and he slung it and struck the Philistine in his forehead, so that the stone sank into his forehead, and he fell on his face to the earth.*
>
> *1 Samuel 17:46-49*

Jewish legend tells us that on the day of the battle, Goliath was so disgusted and amused at the sight of tiny little David running to meet him, that he threw his head backwards and started laughing at David. As he laughed, his helmet jerked backward, revealing his forehead. Just at that moment, David's stone came piercing through his skull! Here was Goliath all decked out in armor, and the one place where it mattered - his forehead - was exposed at exactly the right moment to receive the divinely directed stone! Not only did David **say it**, he also **did it**. Alleluia! David never compared Goliath with himself. He compared him with God and beside God, Goliath was insignificant. To men he was a giant, but David just figured that *"If he's that big, then there's really no way I can miss!"*

3. RECEIVE IT

Now that Goliath was dead, David took Goliath's own sword and relieved him of his head! (1 Samuel 17:50-54) He had said he would do it; he had proceeded to do it; and now David **received** the victory and all the rewards that King Saul had promised to the person who killed Goliath. All the things he had said he was going to do, he set out to do. One step after another, God opened the way for him to **receive** the victory.

4. TELL IT

After the battle has been fought and won, make sure you do not forget to *tell it*! That means share the testimony of what God has done for you with others, and give Him the praise and the glory. *Tell it* so your friends can be encouraged. *Tell it* so others can know that what God has done for you, He can do for them too. In 1 Samuel 18:6, even the women helped David to *tell it*. They came out dancing and singing about the wonderful victory that God had given him.

Toppling the "giant" of sickness

Life is a fight, and those who want to win in life must do exactly what David did. In fact, you will find the same pattern of saying it; doing it; receiving it and telling it, often repeated in the Bible. Read the story of the woman with the issue of blood in the book of Mark chapter 5.

First of all she said it, "If I touch the hem of Jesus' garment, I will be healed."

Secondly, she did it. She found a way to reach Jesus and touch his garment, even though there were many obstacles that could have prevented her from doing it. She was very weak from years of bleeding and could easily have been trampled by the crowd around Jesus. The Law of Moses declared her unclean because of her bleeding. Accordingly, she was prohibited from leaving her home and mixing with *clean* people. By coming out, and breaching this law, she risked the punishment of public stoning. To make matters worse, one of the people who could authorize her stoning, Jairus, was standing right next to Jesus, the person she wanted to touch! This woman however, would not be denied. Yes, she saw all the obstacles in her way, but she wanted that giant of sickness in her life dead, and she was willing to do whatever it took!

Thirdly she received it. Not only did she say she was going to touch Jesus, she proceeded to do it, and when she did it, praise God, she received her healing!

Finally, she told it. After she received her miracle of healing, she shared her testimony with the whole crowd and everyone was blessed by it, and we are still being blessed by it today.

Jesus told the woman that was healed of the issue of blood that her faith had made her whole. If her faith could make her whole, if her faith could cause her, despite all the odds, to persevere until her "giant" of sickness was slain, then so can yours. By faith in God's word and His covenant with every descendant of Abraham, David was able to boldly say that he would kill his giant. He then proceeded to do it, receive it, and tell it.

Today, we are in covenant with God through Jesus Christ. Hebrews 8:6 states that this new covenant is a better one than the Abrahamic covenant, and is based on better promises. How much more then should we, as believers, rise up to our full potential in Christ? It doesn't matter how big or how bad your "giant" might look, you are more that a conqueror through Christ who loves you and won the victory for you. Rise up in bold faith, and refuse to be intimidated by any loud-mouthed giant! All you have to do is say it, do it, receive it, and tell it! Glory to God!

Chapter Seven
FREEDOM FROM FEAR

How did mankind become subject to fear and how can we be free from it? In the book of Genesis chapter 3 we read the story of the fall of man in the Garden of Eden. We learn of how Adam and Eve disobeyed God and the results that followed. God had instructed them not to eat the fruit of the tree of the knowledge of good and evil, for they would die if they ate it. Unfortunately (to say the least!) for them and for us, they disobeyed God.

> *And they heard the sound of the Lord God walking in the garden in the cool of the day, and Adam and his wife hid themselves from the presence of the Lord God among the trees of the garden.*
> *Then the Lord God called to Adam and said to him, "Where are you?"*
> *So he said, "I heard Your voice in the garden, and I was afraid because I was naked; and I hid myself."*
>
> *Genesis 3:8-10*

Adam and Eve disobeyed God and by so doing, sold themselves over to Satan's dominion. They, who had previously fellowshipped freely with the Lord, were suddenly afraid in His presence and ran to hide when they heard His voice. God knew that they had sinned. He knew why and where they were hiding but He still asked, *"Where are you?"* God will always give people the opportunity to confess their sin and repent. Adam however, was now so full of fear that he blamed it all on Eve, the woman God had given him. In other words, everything that happened was all the woman's and God's fault!

They claimed that their reason for hiding was their nakedness. Nakedness was no reason to run from God; after all He knew them inside out. What they were really saying was that they were now stripped of the glory of God that had previously covered them. Man had sinned and come short of the glory of God (Romans 3:23). Adam didn't know that he was running away from the very One who was the answer to his problem. God was not his problem, He was his answer. God came into the garden that day not to condemn man, but to rescue him.

The origin of fear
Man sinned and broke fellowship with God and fear was the result. When Adam sinned, he died spiritually, for God had told him that he would surely die if he ate the forbidden fruit. Notice that he died spiritually, not physically, on the day he ate the fruit. Spiritual death means separation from God, and that separation from God led him to fear God and eventually everything else. From that day on mankind became subject to fear. That is why nobody has to teach a child how to be afraid. Even babies experience fear. If you take each of the letters in the word FEAR, you can accurately define it – **F**alse **E**vidence

<u>A</u>ppearing <u>R</u>eal. That is what fear is. Fear can also be defined as the apprehension or the expectation of evil.

> *Inasmuch then as the children have partaken of flesh and blood, He Himself likewise shared in the same, that through death He might destroy him who had the power of death, that is, the devil, and release those who through fear of death were all their lifetime subject to bondage.*
>
> *Hebrews 2:14-15*

"Fear of death" does not merely refer to people being afraid of death, but also means that fear is the offspring of death. The day man died spiritually, is the same day that spiritual death's offspring, fear, started to hold man in bondage. Praise God, the passage above also tells us that Christ has released us from Satan's bondage, therefore no believer should be bound in any area of his or her life.

When we become born again children of God, we don't receive automatic immunity from fear. Situations will always arise in which fear attacks us, and so we need to learn how to deal with it. Do not confuse this fear with what the Bible calls "the fear of the Lord", or the reverential fear of God. The reverential fear of God prolongs life and brings peace, health and wholeness. It is different from the fear of tornadoes, rattlesnakes or things like that. The latter kind of fear brings torment and destruction.

Characteristics of fear

Fear is not an emotion, but it will influence your emotions. Fear is not a feeling, but it will influence your feelings. The Bible tells us that fear is a spirit. *"For God has not given us a spirit of fear, but of power and of love and of a sound mind."* (2 Timothy 1:7) Every time fear attacks you, it wants to cut you off from power, love, and soundness of mind. It wants to cut you off from everything good that comes from God.

Fear is released in the same way that faith is released. If a person is scared they will talk like it and act like it. Likewise, a person who is full of faith, will talk like it and will act like it. Fear brings the devil on the scene in the same way faith brings God on the scene of your life. Satan attacks you with fear, and if you yield to it, he is then able to work against you. In other words, he can only do in your life what you fear he will do.

In the book of Judges chapter 6 God sent an angel to a man called Gideon. The angel addressed Gideon, "*You mighty man of valor*". However, Gideon's opinion of himself was such that he probably thought the mighty man of valor of whom the angel spoke of was someone lurking around waiting to get him! Gideon did not know that **he** was the mighty man of valor whom God wanted to use to deliver Israel from the oppression of the Midianites. He was so full of fear and timidity that he did not know what God had invested in him. We serve a great God who lives inside us, and that is why we can do great things for Him. Fear always prevents you from seeing yourself the way God sees you in Christ. It completely distorts things from what they really are like and gives you an inaccurate perspective of yourself and your situation.

God is our refuge

People are afraid of everything and anything, but God tells us not to fear. In the book of Psalms chapter 46 He gives us every reason not to;

> *God is our refuge and strength, A very present help in trouble. Therefore we will not fear, Even though the earth be removed, And though the mountains be carried into the midst of the sea;*
>
> *Psalm 46:1-2*

What is a refuge? Places of refuge exist today; for example we have wildlife refuges where animals are protected. If you go in there and harm them, the government will come after you. In Old Testament times, Israel had cities of refuge. The law stated that if you killed another human being, you had to be killed. But if you did it accidentally, you could run to one of the cities of refuge and as long as you stayed there, nobody could hurt you or exact revenge against you, you were protected.

Now the Bible tells us that God is **our** refuge. If there is a time that people fear, it is when they are in trouble. But God says He is not just present in time of trouble, but **very present**. Hallelujah! When God is your refuge, you can run into Him for safety. If anyone wants to come against you they have to come against God and defeat Him first! Now, that is a beautiful place to be in.

God for us, God with us, God in us

There are three kinds of relationships God sustains toward man - God is for us, God is with us, and God is in us. Why is God living in me? Is He just a lonely hitchhiker hitchhiking through life with me? No, He is for me, with me and in me to put me over everything I face in life; to enable me to live victoriously in every area of my life. He said in Hebrews 13:5 that He will never leave me nor forsake me. I like the way the Amplified Bible renders that verse, *"He will not leave you orphans"*. Orphans do not have much of a chance, do they? Satan wants to make you see yourself as a helpless orphan, then he can come in and do anything he wants in your life.

In the book of Numbers chapter 13 we find the children of Israel just three days from Canaan, the Promise Land. It was decided that 12 spies should be sent in to spy out Canaan, the land flowing with milk and honey that God was going to give to them.

> *Now they departed and came back to Moses and Aaron and all the congregation of the children of Israel in the Wilderness of Paran, at Kadesh; they brought back word to them and to all the congregation, and showed them the fruit of the land. Then they told him, and said: "We went to the land where you sent us. It truly flows with milk and honey, and this is its fruit. Nevertheless the people who dwell in the land are strong; the cities are fortified and very large; moreover we saw the descendants of Anak there. The Amalekites dwell in the land of the South; the Hittites, the Jebusites, and the Amorites dwell in the mountains; and the Canaanites dwell by the sea and along the banks of the Jordan."*
>
> *Then Caleb quieted the people before Moses, and said, "Let us go up at once and take possession, for we are well able to overcome it."*
>
> *But the men who had gone up with him said, "We are not able to go up against the people, for they are stronger than we." And they gave the children of Israel a bad report ("evil report" in the KJV) of the land which they had spied out, saying, "The land through which we have gone as spies is a land that devours its inhabitants, and all the people whom we saw in it are men of great stature. There we saw the giants[a] (the descendants of Anak came from the giants); and we were like grasshoppers in our own sight, and so we were in their sight."*
>
> *Numbers 13: 26-33*

This is the land God had been telling them about since they were back in Egypt. Whenever God spoke to them about Canaan He never said anything about giants being there. If God is on your side what difference does it make how many giants there are in the land? Ten of the twelve spies returned with a discouraging report about the unconquerable giants in Canaan. The people had started to despair over this report when Caleb tried to still them in Numbers 14:9, *"Only do not rebel against the Lord, nor fear the people of the land, for they are our bread; their protection has departed from them, and the Lord is with us. Do not fear them."* His words only enraged them further.

Twelve spies went into the land and saw the same things, how then did ten of them come back with an evil report? God simply was not put into the equation. As long as the devil can make you see yourself facing your situation without God, then he has you in a place where fear will rule your life. The Bible calls the ten spies' report evil because their report gave no regard to God or what He had promised to do on their behalf. Fear made them see things in a false light. From Satan's perspective, they saw themselves as insects. That is fear in full manifestation - false evidence about reality, apprehension of, and confident expectation of evil.

What would the giants and armies in Canaan be a type of in your circumstance; what would they represent? They could represent a problem you have been trying to solve for years, or bad habits or addictions. They could represent any satanic opposition or hindrance in your life. I have found it to be true in my life (and the lives of other believers) that when God reveals to me what He wants me to do, He doesn't usually tell me the difficulties I will encounter while doing it. As it was in the Israelites' case, what difference does it make whether there are giants, obstacles or challenges along the way? Since God is the one fighting the battle on our behalf, our victory is assured every time! Hallelujah! God is for us, He is with us and we are never alone. We are more than conquerors because of Jesus.

Fear is contagious
In the book of Numbers chapter 14 we see the effect of the ten spies' fearful words on the rest of the nation:

> *So all the congregation lifted up their voices and cried, and the people wept that night. And all the children of Israel complained against Moses and Aaron, and the whole congregation said to them, "If only we had died in the land of Egypt! Or if only we had died in this wilderness!*
>
> *Numbers 14:1-2*

The whole nation was now gripped with fear.

In our world today, negative information and statistics abound in the news of violent crimes, financial losses, and many other discouraging things. After hearing all that kind of negativity, people come away thinking, "*Things are really bad. I could be next.*" Where is God in that equation? What difference does it make if 5,000 people are estimated to go bankrupt this year, or if 10,000 people are expected to lose their homes? The vast majority of people won't, and why shouldn't I be among those who don't? Looking at natural evidence, zeroing in and focusing on it, will only make you lose your confidence in God. Bad things are happening around us all the time and we are surrounded by people who constantly speak in fear. Fear is contagious and that is why we need to be careful about what we listen to and what we focus on.

Most people upon hearing the news that 50% of the workforce is going to be laid off, would immediately start saying, *"What am I going to do, I know for sure that I'm going to be one of those who get laid off."* In effect they are calling those things which do not exist yet, as though they already did. That is exactly the same way faith works. Though I may not have any money, I can boldly declare that *"My God abundantly supplies all my needs"*. When you talk like that, people get angry with you and accuse of you of being in denial and refusing to face reality. Nobody however, gets upset when you speak words of doubt, fear, or failure, because that's normal for most people. They are already used to living in fear and unbelief.

Know God's love, know no fear

There is no fear in love; but perfect love casts out fear because fear has torment (or punishment).

1 John 4:18

How true it is that fear causes people to live in torment. Christians who are full of fear and who believe that anything bad could happen to them at any moment are not assured of God's love. Furthermore verse 16 of 1 John 4 says, *"And we have known and believed the love that God has for us."* So then it is necessary to not only know that God loves you, but to also believe that He does so. Many believers live like God only loved them enough to get them saved and now He has left them to make it the rest of the way on their own!

Yes, we hear of terrible things happening to people all the time, but we should be able to stop and say, *"Thank You Lord for loving me so much, that according to Psalm 91 You have given Your angels charge over me to keep me in all my ways. I believe You are going to warn me of impending danger"*. That is the way we should think and talk when we know and believe the love of God. Most Christians would probably get mad at you for daring to talk like that and ask, "Who do you think you are? Are you better than brother so-and-so who had something bad happen to him?" No, I am not saying I am better than brother so-and-so. I am only saying God loves me and I am going to be more conscious of that than the fact that the devil hates me. I refuse to live my life in fear of what terrible things might or might not happen.

It has been said that there are about 365 "fear nots" in the Bible, one "fear not" for each day of the year! Fear not, because fear is confidence in the devil's ability to bring calamity to your life. But faith is confidence in what God **can and will** do for you. According to Psalm 91:15 even in the time of trouble, He will be with you, deliver you and honour you.

The many faces of fear

Sometimes fear latches itself onto people as a result of negative past experiences. We all have to watch out in this area. I remember one December when I traveled back to Nigeria. As I was preparing for that trip, I kept feeling uneasy. Something was not quite right, but I didn't know what it was, so all I could do was pray and pray. On Christmas Eve I arrived back in Lagos where I was staying, from a day's trip to another city in Nigeria where I had gone to pick up some valuable personal items that I had kept in storage there. I was planning to take these items back with me to North America.

As I parked in front of the house late that night, I felt impressed to leave all my belongings in the car. However, I resisted that impression, thinking the very idea to be absurd. I took all my things into the house and went to sleep. The next morning, my sister came to wake me up to join the rest of the family for a time of prayer. I initially declined the invitation, wanting to get some more sleep, but I felt a prompting inside me to get up, so eventually I did and went down to join them. Am I ever glad that I did! No sooner than I left that room, than the roof caved in on the bed on which I was sleeping, and the whole room was engulfed in flames! Unknown to us, a fire had begun in the adjoining apartment and had spread through the roof to the room in which I was sleeping. Unfortunately, I lost all my belongings in the fire, but thankfully no one was hurt and the fire was contained to that room alone.

As far as I was concerned the devil had tried his best and missed, but he wasn't through with me yet. On my return journey to North America, I got up to use the restroom in the plane. When I tried to unlock the restroom door, it jammed and for a few moments I could not open the door. Suddenly I was gripped with fear and was tempted to panic. Something seemed to come over me in that moment and I recognized it as the spirit of fear. Praise God the Word and Spirit of God rose up within me, and immediately I said, "*No Satan, you are not going to put this on me in the name of Jesus!*" The memory of my close shave with a fiery death just a few days earlier was still so fresh in me, and Satan was trying to use that as an opportunity to fill my life with fear.

Right here is where a lot of people lose the battle. You do not deal with fear by hoping it goes away, but by rebuking it in the name of Jesus. That's why God has given us authority in Christ. From that moment in the restroom until now, I could have been suffering panic attacks. I probably would never have been able to lock a restroom door again, and the fear would have been growing bigger all the time. Unfortunately, many people actually live like that, held captive by one fear or the other.

Fear manifests itself in many forms, and that is why people suffer from so many different kinds of phobias. Some people have been healed and are afraid that they will lose their healing one day. Others have attempted something and failed at it. The failure was so devastating that they never want to try again. That fear of failure is seeking to limit their future potential in Christ. Maybe you have been divorced and are now remarried, and now you are afraid that your new spouse will do the same thing that your first spouse did. Do not give in to fear! Fear is a spirit, so speak to it in the name of Jesus. Jesus came to set us free from every form of satanic bondage, and no believer should be bound by fear.

It is the privilege of every born again child of God to be free from fear. If you have not done so already, the first thing you need to do is to receive Jesus as your Lord and Saviour by praying the salvation prayer located at the last page of this book. Now, whenever you notice fear trying to attack you in any area of your life, immediately rebuke the fear in the name of Jesus. Satan has no choice but to flee. Find scriptures that apply to your situation, and speak the Word of God to it. May God richly bless you as you live free from fear and all satanic bondage from this day forward!

Chapter Eight
WHAT YOU SEE IS WHAT YOU GET

The Bible is God's vehicle for communicating to us His thoughts about us, and His will for our lives. When God speaks from His Word, He expects us to use our eyes of faith to see our lives lining up with His will. That's why He said, in Proverbs 4:20, "*My son, give attention to my words; Incline your ear to my sayings. Do not let them depart from your eyes; Keep them in the midst of your heart; For they are life to those who find them, And health to all their flesh.*" When the Word departs from your eyes, doubt can then enter in. Doubt will cause the vision you have inside you to start changing or fading.

> *Where there is no revelation (or vision), the people cast off restraint; But happy is he who keeps the law (or Word of God).*
>
> Proverbs 29:18

When a woman is pregnant, she expects to deliver a healthy baby, and this expectation will guide how she lives. She may love to run, but you won't see her competing in a 100-metre race. Why? Because she has a vision of motherhood, she is putting restraints on herself, and is doing everything she can to protect that vision. Likewise, we must do the same when we receive a vision from the Word of God.

Another word the Bible uses for "vision" is "hope". Your vision will create expectancy in you, and it will restrain you from doing certain things. Because you are expecting God to confirm His Word on your behalf, you will not be out in the world sinning and doing things that will get you out of fellowship with Him. That Word-based vision, which you see so clearly in the womb of your spirit, is restraining you from wrong living.

Begin with a vision

In Genesis 13, God told Abraham that He would give him all the land that he could see. Abraham had to go 'see' the land, and had to walk over it, in order to possess it. You have to have a vision of what you want. Have it sculptured solid inside you, strong and clear. See it like you could almost taste it, then begin to declare it with your mouth.

Genesis chapter 11 provides a good illustration. The people had decided they were going to build a tower all the way to heaven. Even with our modern day technology we haven't aspired to such a feat! These people however, had something going for them.

> *Indeed the people are one and they all have one language, and this is what they begin to do; now nothing that they propose to do will be withheld from them.*
>
> *Genesis 11:6*

"Propose" here, means "imagine". When you imagine something you "see" it. Today when we build, we start with a blueprint. We don't know if those folks had one like we use today, but we do know that they had a blueprint of whatever they were going to build engraved inside of them. Not only did they have one language, but also they were united in purpose. God Himself testified that nothing would stop these people from doing whatever they imagined to do, and so He had to intervene.

From this we can learn how important it is to first start with a vision, and then a way will be made to realize that vision. For example, during one of Michael Jordan's basketball games he made over 55 points including three-pointer baskets! When asked at the end of the game how he thought he had been able to accomplish this, his response was that he had imagined the basket to be so big and wide, that there was just no way that he could miss!

In Genesis 11, God intervened by giving those tower builders different languages. Suddenly they couldn't communicate with each other. More importantly, that image of the tower they had inside them could no longer be enhanced, and they had to abandon their efforts to build.

That's exactly how doubt works. Contradictory words, feelings and circumstances, come to challenge the image of victory, healing, or blessing that you have inside your heart, and the image then begins to wane and die, ultimately leading to defeat.

David sees things differently

A case in point is the story of David in 1 Samuel 17. David was sent to take supplies to his older brothers at the warfront. He arrived there to hear Goliath the giant, challenging Israel's army.

> *And a champion went out from the camp of the Philistines, named Goliath, from Gath, whose height was six cubits and a span (about [9] feet [9] inches)... Then he stood and cried out to the armies of Israel, and said to them, 'Why have you come out to line up for battle? Am I not a Philistine, and you the servants of Saul? Choose a man for yourselves, and let him come down to me. If he is able to fight with me and kill me, then we will be your servants. But if I prevail against him and kill him, then you shall be our servants and serve us.' And the Philistine said, 'I defy the armies of Israel this day; give me a man, that we may fight together.' When Saul and all Israel heard these words of the Philistine, they were dismayed and greatly afraid.*
>
> 1 Samuel 17:4, 8-11

David arrived with the supplies, heard the same words, but his response was totally different.

> "*And all the men of Israel, when they saw the man, fled from him and were dreadfully afraid. So the men of Israel said, 'Have you seen this man who has come up? Surely he has come up to defy Israel; and it shall be that the man who kills him the king will enrich with great riches, will give him his daughter, and give his father's house exemption from taxes in Israel.' Then David spoke to the men who stood by him, saying,... 'For who is this uncircumcised Philistine, that he should defy the armies of the living God?'*"
>
> 1 Samuel 17: 24-26

Why did Goliath's word inspire fear in everyone else, but faith in David? What was the difference? Notice the way David addressed Goliath as an "uncircumcised Philistine". What did he mean by that? In Genesis chapter 17 Abraham cut covenant with God by circumcision. By the same token, everyone in the natural lineage of Abraham, entered into that same covenant through circumcision. God had promised Abraham that anyone who blessed him, He would bless, and anyone who cursed him, He would curse. David realized that because he was a circumcised descendant of Abraham, he had all the benefits of Abraham's covenant with God. All of Israel did too, but they just didn't believe it or walk in the light of it. Goliath had not entered into any such covenant with God, and so he was defenseless against David and God!

It wasn't a matter of having the wherewithal or the weaponry to face the opposing army. God was the One who would fight for them. David just measured the image and understanding he had of who God was against Goliath and the Philistine army. **David looked at Goliath but did not see him as a giant - beside God nobody is a giant and nothing is gigantic!** Alleluia! The rest of Israel compared Goliath to their limited selves. They saw themselves as little and Goliath as huge. But David took Goliath and compared him to God. He didn't even put himself in the picture, he was putting Goliath against his God, and Goliath was no match for God.

The goliath in your life

Goliath is a type for us today, representing anything that the devil is using to harass you. You may see your $100,000 debt as **huge**, especially when all you have coming in is $800 a month. When you are sitting at your table, looking at your bills, compare them to your Almighty God. Take those bills and compare them to the riches of God in Christ Jesus. All of a sudden, your bills will start shrinking! That's why it is so important what you focus your eyes and attention on. Fear enters into our hearts when we begin to focus on physical evidence.

What if your doctor tells you that you have cancer? You break the news to your family and friends and they sink into despair as they start telling you of all the people they know who have died from cancer. Suddenly the cancer starts growing bigger in your mind, into a huge unstoppable monster. All the doctors in the world can't stop it! What you need to do is put the cancer beside Jesus and His healing power. When you start to look at the situation in the proper perspective, the cancer won't look so big anymore. Instead it will begin to shrink, and Jesus will ultimately dwarf it out of existence!

Act in faith, don't pray in doubt

David had built a big, powerful, image of God in his heart. He didn't just build that image the day he met Goliath. His image of God was developed over all those years he had spent taking care of sheep, singing psalms to the Lord and meditating on the Word of God. When the enemy's attack came against that image, David did not give in to fear like the others did. He didn't even stop to pray about what he should do. Often times when Christians are going through a crisis, they stop to pray and seek God's will on what to do, but in some situations doing that can actually be an act of unbelief.

For example, if someone told you they wanted to get saved, would you first stop and pray to ask Jesus if He wants to save that person? No. You already know that the Word of God says that salvation is for "whosoever" (John 3:16). Likewise, if someone were to ask for prayer for healing, do we need to go pray and ask God if He wants to heal that person? No. We already know that in Acts 10:38, the Bible says, "God anointed **Jesus of Nazareth** with the Holy Spirit and with power, **who went about doing good and healing all** who were oppressed by the devil…"

It was the same way with David. He didn't need to pray and ask God what he should do about Goliath. He knew what the Word said about the benefits of his covenant with God through Abraham. All David needed to do was act on that covenant in faith. The saddest thing about the whole situation was that every person in Israel had as much right to that covenant as David did. But he was the only person who benefited from it. Thank God he was in Israel that day, otherwise the army of Israel would have been wiped out! **How sad that they had more faith in Goliath's words than in God's.**

Similarly, many Christians have more confidence in what the doctor has told them than what Jesus has said in His Word. The doctor might tell you that you have only two months to live. But Jesus will tell you to go ahead and live another 80 years if you want to! That doesn't mean that doctors are wrong. **You should acknowledge the physical facts, but use God's word to overcome them. Take God's report as a higher authority that can, and will change the doctor's report!** David knew that any Israelite could easily kill Goliath, and he couldn't believe that nobody was accepting King Saul's reward offer! And so he accepted Goliath's challenge.

Faith-filled words

Immediately after declaring his bold words, David's oldest brother, Eliab, opposed him (I Samuel 17:28). The same thing may happen to you. There are times when you may take a bold stand and speak faith-filled words from the Bible. People will come against you, especially fellow Christians, and say that you are proud. But actually it has nothing to do with you or pride; it's all about your confidence in your covenant with God through Jesus.

> *Then (David) turned from (Eliab) toward another and said the same thing;... Now when the words which David spoke were heard, they reported them to Saul; and he sent for him."*
>
> 1 Samuel 17:30-31

There is no point in trying to explain what you believe and what you are doing to people who are not going to receive it. Just leave them alone, turn from them like David did. You can't afford to cast your pearls before swine!

When you were little, did you ever get together with other kids and tell scary stories? What effect did that have on your body - chills, goose bumps? Some people can hear bad news and immediately get diarrhea. If bad words can do that, think of what wholesome, faith-filled words can do! If bad news can cause people to collapse, then healing words from the Bible will build strength, and put life and energy back into your body. That's why we need to constantly feed on God's Word.

Keep the fight on God's level

> *Then David said to Saul, "Let no man's heart fail because of him (Goliath); your servant will go and fight with this Philistine."*
> *And Saul said to David, "You are not able to go against this Philistine to fight with him; for you are a youth, and he a man of war from his youth."*
>
> 1 Samuel 17:32-33

Here Saul brings the situation down to the mere human level, into the natural realm. People will challenge your bold stand of faith again and again asking; "who do you think you are?" But remember, it is not you, or your background or where you come from that matters, but what God says.

David however puts the situation back on God's level, into the supernatural realm, when he says in verse 37;

> Moreover David said, "The Lord, who delivered me from the paw of the lion and from the paw of the bear, He will deliver me from the hand of this Philistine."
> And Saul said to David, "Go, and the Lord be with you!"
>
> *1 Samuel 17:37*

As far as David was concerned, it didn't depend on him or his ability. He was basing his victory on the supernatural ability of God.

And so with King Saul's permission, David went to meet Goliath, dressed as a shepherd boy, with no armour or weapon other than a slingshot. The sight of David made Goliath so angry that he said to David, " *'Am I a dog, that you come to me with sticks?' And (Goliath) the Philistine cursed David by his gods."* You can't stop the circumstances, the symptoms, the bills, or whatever, from talking to you. You can't even stop Satan from talking to you. But as soon as he's through talking, you better have something to say in return. Interrupt him if you like, but make sure you boldly declare what you know will happen, what God will do for you!

Talk back to your circumstances like David did in verse 45;

> Then David said to the Philistine, "You come to me with a sword, with a spear, and with a javelin. But I come to you in the name of the Lord of hosts, the God of the armies of Israel, whom you have defied.
>
> *1 Samuel 17:45*

Saul had given him his armour to use, but David had to put it down because he hadn't proved or tested it. David came against Goliath in the name of the Lord, the name of the Lord was the weapon he had proved.

Psalm 20:1 says, *"May the name of the God of Jacob defend you"*. Thank God we have the name of Jesus to defend us today! All that the Father's name represents has been put in the name of Jesus for us. Salvation, healing, protection, provision, all are in the name of Jesus. The Bible tells us that whatever we do in word or deed, we are to do it in the name of Jesus.

Jewish legend tells us that Goliath was completely covered in metal armour. When David ran towards him, Goliath laughed. As he laughed his head jerked back and his helmet slid up. Just then David released a stone from his sling and hit him right between the eyes. That was supernatural! God made a way for the victory David had conceived in his heart to take place (*see 1 Samuel 17:46-49*). *"So David prevailed over the Philistine with a sling and a stone, and struck the Philistine and killed him..."*

The road to glory

In 2 Corinthians 4:17 Paul refers to all the persecution he suffered as **"light affliction"** - the stonings, the beatings with rods, etc. His perception of his sufferings was obviously different from what most people would have had in the same situation. In the natural what was happening to him was very painful, but he said, *"For our **light affliction**, which is but for a moment, is working for us a far more exceeding and eternal **weight of glory**..."* Paul concluded that the light affliction, the persecution and turmoil, which Satan was trying to use to hinder his ministry and ultimately destroy him, was merely working the way gasoline works in your car to take you from one point to another. The **light** affliction was working to take him to a **weighty** place of glory! He refused to see his situation the way the enemy wanted him to.

Whatever you may be facing, remember that the enemy is trying to use it for your destruction, but God can use it as raw material to bring blessings and glory to you. But how does the affliction work to produce glory? The answer is in verse 18 of 2 Corinthians 4, *"while we do not look at the things which are seen..."* David refused to look at, or focus on Goliath's intimidating physical attributes. He focused on God. In other words, when you start looking at your circumstances, the power of God cannot work for you.

> *While we do not look at the things which are seen, but at the things which are not seen. For the things which are seen are temporary, but the things which are not seen are eternal.*
>
> *2 Corinthians 4:18.*

The things that cannot be seen, are the visions of victory that you have inside your heart. Focusing on them will bring you to the glorious outcome God desires for you.

Meditate on God's word daily. We all meditate on something everyday. But if you don't consciously choose to meditate on God's word, the devil will be sure to supply you with plenty of food for thought! Meditation will produce a clear vision of God's Word inside you. Let that vision fill your mind and your heart. Cut off anything that attempts to change or modify it. It may be friends, the news, the TV or whatever. If it's giving you a bad report - stay away from it!

Don't allow your vision from God to be tampered with. It doesn't matter how you feel or don't feel; what people say or don't say. The only things the enemy can use against you are your thoughts and your words. If he can get you destabilized in your thinking, he can get you to change and abort your vision. Remember that what you see, is what you get!

Chapter Nine
WHOSE REPORT WILL YOU BELIEVE?

Everything you and I enjoy today is as a result of what Jesus purchased for us at Calvary. The people in the Old Testament got blessed by God because of what Jesus was going to do. We are blessed today because of what He has done.

What we call the Gospel of Christ is not just the books of Matthew, Mark, Luke and John, it is all the books in the New Testament. This gospel (or the good news) is the revelation that Paul taught in his epistles. Paul's teaching can be divided into three main parts. Firstly, who we are in Christ, what God did for us in Christ. Secondly, what the Holy Spirit through the agency of the Word is doing and can do in the life of the believer. And thirdly, the present day ministry of the Lord Jesus Christ. The apostle Paul taught that because we are born again and blood washed, we are new creatures in Christ, thus we should live like it, and not live like the world.

The ministry of Jesus Today

Let us now look at what Jesus did for us and how that affects us today. A non-Christian might ask, "Jesus lived about 2000 years ago. Of what relevance is that man who lived so long ago to my life today?" Answering that question is what the gospel is all about.

> *Who has believed our report? And to whom has the arm of the Lord been revealed?*
>
> Isaiah 53: 1

This is a rhetorical question, the answer being contained in it. The arm of the Lord is revealed to those who believe the report. If you don't believe the report, then the arm of the Lord is NOT going to be revealed to you. "The arm of the Lord" stands for the power of God, His divine ability on our behalf. When people came to Jesus, they put a demand on the ability of God that was in Him. Today people are still wanting to put a demand on His ability, and want God to move on their behalf. That is why we are here, we in whom He lives can minister in His power!

Jesus in the Old Testament

Someone once asked if you could teach about Jesus from the Old Testament. Jesus is all over the Old Testament. In the book of Acts chapter 28 the Romans were questioning Paul concerning the new revelation he was preaching. The Bible says that Paul then preached Jesus to them from the law of Moses and all through the prophets. In the early days of the church, all they had were the books of the Old Testament, and that is what they preached from. But thank God today we have the Old and New Testaments, and we can teach about Jesus from both of them.

He is despised and rejected of men; a man of sorrows, and acquainted with grief: and we hid as it were our faces from him; he was despised, and we esteemed him not.

Isaiah 53: 3

In this passage, prophet Isaiah is seeing down the road, seeing what was going to happen to Jesus many centuries later. He is writing about Jesus' death and what He was coming to do on the cross at Calvary.

The Old Testament contains many prophetic writings like these about Jesus. In the book of Psalms chapter 22 you see Jesus dying on the cross, *"My God, my God, why have you forsaken me?"* In the 23rd Psalm we see Jesus as our shepherd, while in Psalm 24 He is the King of kings, and Lord of lords.

The Bible is a legal document. People have said that it is the best document on jurisprudence that there is, and it establishes God's covenant with man. Jesus is very God and very Man. By this we mean that He is fully God and fully Man; He is not 50/50. The Bible calls Him the Son of Man and the Son of God. Thus Jesus alone qualified to pay the price for our sin, as all mankind had been condemned as sinners when Adam sinned. No human being could pay the awful price, so God had to make provision. But at the same time it could not be just all God. Jesus was the perfect Lamb of God, but He became a man so He could identify with us.

The power of Identification

We see the power of identification all the time. In high school whenever your favourite school team went to play ball they represented you. When they won, you said "We won!" You didn't play, but you identified with the team and told everyone that *you* won! That is identification! And so Jesus, though He was God, became a man and identified with us, and that act qualified Him to become our substitute. Jesus was our substitute in His sacrificial death, but we were there too.

> *And I, if I am lifted up from the earth, will draw all peoples to Myself.*
>
> *John 12:32*

We usually think of this verse in terms of praise and worship. But Jesus wasn't talking about praise and worship here, for the very next verse says;

> *This He said, signifying by what death He would die.*
>
> *John 12:33*

When Jesus was suspended on that cross between the heavens and the earth, He drew all humanity into Himself. You were there in Him. Because He was our substitute, we were there.

When you look at the cross, don't just see Jesus dying. He did not die for Himself; you should see yourself there. The death, burial and resurrection of Jesus was a group picture of the whole of humanity - suffering, dying, humanity. When you first saw the group picture of your high school graduating class, the very first person you wanted to see was yourself. Similarly when you look at the cross, you should immediately see yourself there, for you were in Christ and you died when He died!

Remember the old song, "Were You There When They Crucified My Lord?" Yes, we were in Him when He hung on that cross, in Him when He died, and rose victorious from the grave! The Bible calls Jesus the second and the last Adam, for He is the Father of a brand new race of people called "saints". Adam was the father of a fallen race of people called "sinners".

Jesus died spiritually

When Jesus went to Calvary, He paid the penalty for sin and all the consequences of sin. If He only paid the penalty for sin without paying for its consequences, then He did not finish His job; He did not do a good job. Then there is something left for us to do. But Jesus finished His work. He did an excellent job upon which nobody can improve, He paid for our sin and the consequences of sin. If there was no sin, would there be sickness? No. If there was no sin, would there be poverty, oppression, problems? No. All these are the result of sin, and in dealing with sin, Jesus dealt with them. Alleluia!

> *Surely he hath borne our griefs, and carried our sorrows: yet we did esteem him stricken, smitten of God, and afflicted.*
> *But he was wounded for our transgressions, he was bruised for our iniquities: the chastisement of our peace was upon him; and with his stripes we are healed.*
> *Yet it pleased the Lord to bruise Him; He has put Him to grief. When You make His soul an offering for sin, He shall see His seed, He shall prolong His days, and the pleasure of the Lord shall prosper in His hand.*
>
> Isaiah 53:4-5, 10

The Bible says that Jesus was smitten (or struck down) of God. The Roman soldiers didn't do that. "He was bruised for our iniquities"; it pleased God to bruise (or crush) Him, for He saw ahead the benefits that would accrue to you and I, our redemption. The soldiers inflicted some things on Jesus outwardly, but they could not put our sins on Him. Only God could do that. Hanging on that cross, all our sin and all its effects were put on Jesus - that was the bruising. God put our sin, sickness, disease, lack, sorrow, pain, everything the devil had to offer, on Him so that we could be free!

We were spiritually dead. The moment Adam sinned, humanity died. If Jesus took our place then He must have died spiritually. The book of Isaiah chapter 52 talks about His "deaths"; He didn't just die physically.

The Bible calls Jesus the first begotten (or first born) from the dead. He was not raised from the dead, He was resurrected. Lazarus was raised from the dead by Jesus, but he is not called the first begotten from the dead. Jesus went to the region of the damned, where you and I were supposed to go, and He was the first to come back from there. Thus He became the first begotten from the dead; the first person to be born again.

Jesus bore sickness and disease

Let us look at the words '"griefs" and "sorrows" in Isaiah 53:3-4. "Griefs" is translated from the Hebrew word "chole", which means sickness, disease or malady (see Strong's Concordance). "Chole" is used again in Deuteronomy 7:15, 28:59 and 61, 1Kings 17:17; 2 Kings 1:2, 8:8; and 2 Chronicles 21:15. In each of these verses the word is translated "sickness", and in 2 Chronicles 16:12, "chole" is translated "disease". "Sorrows" on the other hand is from the Hebrew word "makob", which means "pain", "inconvenience". In Job 14:22 and 33:19, "makob" is translated as "pain".

Bearing all this in mind, let us look back at Isaiah 53:3-4, and substitute the words "sickness" and "disease" for the word "griefs", and substitute "sorrows" with "pain". Those who lived when the King James Version of the

Bible was published may have understood "griefs" and "sorrows" to mean sickness and pain, but today those words do not convey the same meaning.

Once again looking forward to a future time, prophet Isaiah wrote in Isaiah 53:5, "*…..and with His stripes we are healed.*" But Peter in 1 Peter 2:24, looking back to the past declares, "*….by His stripes we **were** healed.*" In every hospital room in this city there is someone who is healed already, but doesn't know it. Why? Because they have not believed the report of the Lord, and the arm of the Lord is not revealed unto them.

Jesus healed them all

In the book of Matthew chapter 8 we see Jesus ministering healing. He was always ministering to someone, or going to minister to someone, or just coming from ministering to someone. Erroneously some have said that God put sickness on them to teach them a lesson, or to demonstrate to others how much they can endure. Others have claimed that God took their mother or baby away before their time, because He needed another voice in the heavenly choir. That is simply spiritual mumbo jumbo!

This is their way of trying to console themselves in the face of loss, or over some defeat they have experienced. If the devil beat you, admit it, and decide to stand against him the next time.

Jesus went to Peter's home and ministered healing to his mother-in-law (Matthew 8:14). And in the evening He healed *all* that were sick (Matthew 8:16). He never refused to heal anyone. Even those who were unsure of His will for them were healed. If you had been one of the sick there that day, you would have been healed. He healed all their sick, which means that God wants *all* to be healed today too!

The book of Matthew chapter 8 explains why Jesus healed all the sick. Quoting from Isaiah 53:4, but instead of "griefs" and "sorrows", the verse reads thus;

> that it might be fulfilled which was spoken by Isaiah the prophet, saying: "He Himself took our infirmities and bore our sicknesses."
>
> *Matthew 8:17*

So even if you do not believe all I have said up to now, believe the New Testament!

The sick came to Jesus crying, "Jesus, thou son of David, have mercy on me!" Healing therefore must be a mercy. How many is mercy for? All. If mercy is for all, then healing must be for all as well.

Jesus already won

What is a testament? It is a will. Jesus put down His own testament before He died. He made all the promises and provision for every need that could arise. However, a testament only comes into force when the testator dies. So Jesus died, but He rose up from the dead to come and execute His own will; just to see to it that you got whatever He had promised you! If all wills were executed that way, there would be no problems amongst the beneficiaries and heirs.

Thus we see the all encompassing scope of our redemption. We have not only been redeemed from sin, but from all the effects of sin. That doesn't mean that you will live a problem-free life; there is a devil out there who intends to see to it that lots of problems come your way. The good news however is that whatever the problem you face today, Jesus has already taken care of it for you. He won the victory for you.

Think of your favourite team. You didn't get to watch the last game in which they won the championship, but you were told that the scores were 5-0 in their favour. When you watch the replay of the game the next day, one thing is for sure: No matter how good the other team plays, they are not going to win!

Such is the victory Jesus Christ won for us at Calvary. Jesus won our victory over oppression, depression, sickness, lack , and everything that the devil puts on humanity. No matter how tough it gets, he cannot win if you believe the report of the Lord. No matter how good the devil plays, he cannot win because the score has already been determined.

Watch your words

Jesus rose up from the dead and is seated at the right hand of the Father in glory. We believe that, and we talk like that. Let us not talk like the world, for the world has its own language.

You will here people say, "Whenever the flu comes around, you just watch it, I'll be the first to catch it." That is faith in the enemy's ability to work calamity in their lives talking. If layoffs are occurring on the job, you will hear things like, "I just know I'll be next. Though my name wasn't on the last list, I'll be on the next one." Few people in the face of impending layoffs would say, "Thank God I'm not going to lose my job. This will be a good opportunity for me to probably get a raise. Or even if I do lose this job, there's a better one waiting for me because God is on my side!" Do you know people who talk like that? Probably not too many.

Most people have jobs. It is only a tiny percentage that is unemployed. But many have more faith to be in that tiny percentage than to be amongst the majority. Their faith is in the devil and his works, and they exercise that faith by the way they talk. "Inflation is up again; the dollar just keeps going down; things are getting harder. This government is the pits!" Such people have their faith in the things they can see, and the devil likes that.

We should talk like children of God, like those who believe the report of God, His word. If the flu epidemic comes to town, you should say, "Thank God by His stripes I am healed. I claim immunity against that in the name of Jesus, and I plead the blood of Jesus over me and my household. No plague will come near our dwelling."

If the enemy tells you, "I'm going to destroy you", you should be smart enough to know not to go about repeating his words, saying, "Satan is going to destroy me!" We speak the word of the Lord.

A blind man was once asked, "What is worse than being blind?" He answered, "To have sight but no vision." People have the wrong vision about life. When Goliath who stood nine and a half feet tall, came against Israel, the soldiers cried out, "Surely this guy has come to kill us, we are done for!" But when David showed up, he saw an opportunity for promotion; he had a different vision. The men were complaining about how big Goliath was, but David thought, "If he's that big, then there is no way I can miss!"

This is exactly how faith works. What are you seeing about your circumstances? How do you see your future? Whose report are you going to believe, Satan's or God's?

If there was no sin, there would be no defeat. There would be no sickness, disease, lack or anything that could hurt us. Jesus has taken care of all of this. He has taken care of your sin, every problem you are having right now, and every problem you will ever face. God is in covenant with us, He has got the power to help us. Thank you Lord!

If there was a doctor in town who had discovered the cure for cancer, and a woman comes to him and says she is dying of cancer, only to have him turn her away, saying that he doesn't believe he can help her. Yes, he has the cure, but he doesn't want to use it on her. What are people going to think of such a doctor? Not much, I can assure you.

But that is what people say about God. They say He has the power to heal them, the power to deliver them from whatever situation they may be facing, but they are wondering if He will or not. Religious thinking makes people unreasonable when it comes to spiritual things. We who are in covenant with God should put Him in remembrance of His word. Believe the report, and the arm and power of God will be revealed on your behalf!

Chapter Ten
KEEP YOUR MOUTH IN LINE WITH YOUR MIRACLE

Jesus is coming back soon. When He returns, will He find you living by faith, and actively using your faith to fulfil God's will for your life? Will you still be believing God for big things, believing for people to be saved, healed and delivered? In Luke 18:8 Jesus asked if He will find faith in the earth, when He returns.

After we leave this life, faith will still be a factor. 1 Corinthians 13:13 says, *"And now abide faith, hope, love, these three..."* If you do not know how to walk in faith here, you will have to learn in heaven, and probably have to sit in Sunday School over there! God is a faith God. Even when Satan is no longer on the scene, we will have to live by faith. Faith and dependence on the Word of God must consistently be taught for believers to gain victory in every area of their lives.

It is essential then that we get our faith in fighting shape. Is your faith out of shape? Is it fat and flabby? Or, are you one of those Christians who is looking for a way to avoid using their faith altogether? The Bible calls us "believers", therefore by virtue of our new birth, it is our nature to believe. Whether you know it or not, believing God is spiritual work, and all those who desire to live victoriously in Christ, will have to do that work.

Unbelieving believers

Have you ever met a believer who didn't believe? There are lots of them - unbelieving believers! Zacharias in the book of Luke chapter 1, was like one of them. He and his wife Elizabeth had been married for many years and had been unable to have children. They were now old, and their prayers for a child had seemingly gone unanswered. Then one day, an angel appeared to Zacharias, and told him that his prayer had been heard. Zacharias found it hard to believe the angel. At his old age, he seemed to have forgotten about any prayer for a child. God however, does not forget your prayers. Revelation 5:8 says that our prayers are stored in vials or bowls in heaven, and that they are beautiful perfume to the Lord.

> *And when Zacharias saw him, he was troubled, and fear fell upon him.*
> *But the angel said to him, "Do not be afraid, Zacharias, for your prayer is heard; and your wife Elizabeth will bear you a son, and you shall call his name John. And you will have joy and gladness, and many will rejoice at his birth..."*
> *And Zacharias said to the angel, "How shall I know this? For I am an old man, and my wife is well advanced in years."*
>
> Luke 1:12-14, 18

Zacharias questioned the possibility of the angel's words. It appeared that he had long given up on becoming a father. Why did God have to send an angel? Why didn't He just go ahead and let Elizabeth get pregnant? Simply because your prayers being answered has a lot to do with you, not just God. If it was all left up to God, He would just do whatever He wanted to do and wouldn't bother telling anybody about it. God required Zacharias to cooperate, to believe, to have faith, ahead and gave him the word from God. But Zacharias could not believe it and asked for proof.

When people pray to get saved, do they have to pray a desperate and panicky prayer? "O God, save me. Don't let me got to hell!" No. Even though that is the greatest need in anybody's life, they can come calmly to the Lord and pray for salvation, and be born again. Why should any other prayer be different? There could never be any emergency that could supersede that one! Some Christians today are still praying like Zacharias, "O God, prove to me that what You are telling me is the truth. Prove to me that You are not a liar."

God needs your cooperation

And the angel answered and said to him, "I am Gabriel, who stands in the presence of God, and was sent to speak to you and bring you these glad tidings.

Luke 1:19

When Zacharias heard the good news from God, he should have been rejoicing and singing and dancing, not asking for proof. Many today read the Word of God in the same way. They read the very answers to their problems in the Bible but they do not believe it.

As a result of his unbelief, Gabriel told Zacharias in Luke 1:20 that he would be dumb until the child's birth. God needed his cooperation in order to help him. But Zacharias' attitude was such that he could foul up everything with his mouth, and so the angel had to silence him by rendering him dumb. Now he couldn't speak against the miracle that God was about to do. He was not dumb by sickness or disease, but by the power of God coming on him. His speech was restored after his son was born.

Many have actually put themselves into the bad and negative situations they find themselves in because of wrong and sinful talking. People sin a lot with their mouths. The Bible says that anything that is not done in faith, is sin. So, many are sinning all the time and do not even know it! That is what Zacharias was doing, so God had to keep him quiet until the miracle took place. You can either use your mouth to strengthen your faith, or to undermine it.

In the book of Mark chapter 5, Jesus was following Jairus at his request, to his home to heal his sick daughter. Before they reached Jairus' house, a servant came to inform him that his daughter was now dead. Jesus immediately told him "Do not be afraid, only believe." If it was all dependent on Jesus, then He could have handled the situation alone, whether or not Jairus was afraid. But Jairus also had his part to play; Jesus needed his faith to help him. In the same way, He will need your faith to help you. If everything was dependent on God, then the whole world would be saved today, and tomorrow we would all be in heaven!

There are 19 different individual cases of healing that are recorded in the four gospels. In 10 of those cases, the faith of the individual was specifically mentioned as being the initiator of the healing. In the other 9 cases it is inferred. The people were the ones who initiated the miracle. Jesus told the woman with the issue of blood that her faith had made her whole. The same thing is true for you - your faith can make you whole.

Some Christians think that if God wants to heal them, then He will. What if an unbeliever thought that if God wanted to get him born again, then He would? We already know conclusively from the Bible that God wants to save and heal everyone. He has already done His part through the sacrifice of His Son. The issue then is, are you going to believe His Word, and do what it takes to receive what He has already given you. God's part is to see that the Word goes forth. But once you have heard the Word, it is then your turn to make a move. Start putting your faith into action.

Speak only in faith

One of the main ways to put your faith into action is to speak out and declare with your mouth what you believe and are expecting from the Word of God.

In the book of 1 Samuel chapter 17 we read of how David defeated the giant, Goliath. David had confidence in his powerful covenant with God. Without even stopping to pray about it, he boldly declared that he would kill this Goliath who had dared to defy God. He spoke out in faith, and got exactly what he said.

The woman with the issue of blood in the book of Mark chapter 5 heard the good news about Jesus the Healer. She said, "*If I can touch the hem of His garment, I will be made whole.*" She spoke it out. You need to speak out your faith. When you brag on your Father, He will live up to His name!

You may know from His Word that God wants you healed, but how do you release your faith to receive the promised healing that you need? Begin by speaking out the healing scriptures on which you are standing in faith. For example, you can say "God has sent His Word and healed, and delivered me from all destruction (Psalm 107:20). You are the Lord who heals me (Exodus 15:26)."

When things are not going well for you, if you can't say anything good, say nothing at all. Remember when Jairus was told by his servant that his daughter was dead, Jesus immediately instructed him to not be afraid but to only believe. There are times when you need to keep quiet. Do not make faith confessions out of fear - just keep quiet. Let the faith filled words that you have already spoken, begin to take effect. Do not negate them with words of fear and doubt.

Do not question the Word of God

Further on in the book of Luke chapter 1, the angel Gabriel brought a word from God to another person, Mary, the mother of Jesus. This situation however was different from Zacharias'. Whereas he had prayed for a child, Mary had not. She wasn't even married yet.

> *Now in the sixth month the angel Gabriel was sent by God to a city of Galilee named Nazareth, to a virgin betrothed to a man whose name was Joseph, of the house of David. The virgin's name was Mary. And having come in, the angel said to her, "Rejoice, highly favored one, the Lord is with you; blessed are you among women!"*
> *But when she saw him, she was troubled at his saying, and considered what manner of greeting this was. Then the angel said to her, "Do not be afraid, Mary, for you have found favor with God. And behold, you will conceive in your womb and bring forth a Son, and shall call His name Jesus.*
> *Then Mary said to the angel, "How can this be, since I do not know a man?"*
> *And the angel answered and said to her, "The Holy Spirit will come upon you, and the power of the Highest will*

overshadow you; therefore, also, that Holy One who is to be born will be called the Son of God.

Luke 1:26-31, 34-35

Unlike Zacharias, Mary was not questioning the possibility of Gabriel's words. She was simply asking a legitimate question on how to cooperate with the miracle, seeing that she was a virgin and had known no man. This was not a question of doubt or unbelief. It was a question on how to position herself to receive what God was about to do through her.

Every miracle or working of God is the product of the word of God, and the Spirit of God. John 1:14 tells us that the Word become flesh. The word Mary received from the angel, that anointed word became flesh in her by the action of the Holy Spirit. The word of God you receive concerning your healing can become healing in your flesh. The word of God you receive concerning your finances, with the Holy Spirit's anointing coming on it, will bring blessing in that area of your finances. The word of God you receive in any area - depression, family issues, etc. - coming into you with the anointing of the Holy Spirit on it, will produce your miracle.

When the word of God comes, it is always good news, glad tidings. The word 'gospel' means 'good news'. No matter what situation you may find yourself in, the word has good news for you, But you have to receive that word, so that the anointing of the Holy Spirit can come on it, to make it real in your life. If however, you are still questioning and doubting that word, you cannot receive it.

Some Christians have said, "*If Jesus walked into my room, where I was sick on my bed, I know He will heal me.*" But

Jesus already said that "...*where two or three are gathered together in My name, I am there...*" (Matthew 18:20). And, "*I will never leave you nor forsake you.*" (Hebrews 13:15). Therefore, Jesus is here with us today. You do not have to hope that He will specially make a visit to see you. Take the Word literally for what it says. Do not have your faith in the wrong things- waiting until you 'feel' or 'see' something, or until your senses tell you that something is happening. That is where many people lose their miracle over and over again.

Be like Mary

There is more that we can learn from what Mary said and did in her situation.

> Now indeed, Elizabeth your relative has also conceived a son in her old age; and this is now the sixth month for her who was called barren. For with God nothing will be impossible." Then Mary said, "Behold the maidservant of the Lord! Let it be to me according to your word." And the angel departed from her.
>
> Luke 1:36-38

This is the same thing we should say anytime the word of God comes to us; "*Be it unto me according to Your word, O Lord.*" Mary believed it. She received it. Do not sit back with a passive attitude and tell God that HE can do anything He wants to. God cannot do some things except through you. You have something to do with it. Receive the Word actively.

If the richest man in the world told you today that he was going to give you millions of dollars, would you promptly forget it and never think about what he said again? No! You would be spending that money in your head! You would be thinking and talking and acting like a millionaire - all because of the words of a man, who has the financial ability to keep his promise. How much more then, should we take God at His word. God who cannot lie, and who never will.

> *Now Mary arose in those days and went into the hill country with haste, to a city of Judah, and entered the house of Zacharias and greeted Elizabeth.*
> *And Mary remained with her about three months, and returned to her house.*
>
> *Luke 1:39-40, and 56*

Put yourself in Mary's shoes. You are not married and you have been told by an angel that you are going to have a baby out of wedlock. Back then, such a pregnancy constituted a sin, punishable by stoning to death. Mary knew her baby was the result of a supernatural act of God, but nobody else around her knew. Rather than subject herself to people's curious stares, condemning tongues and judgmental attitudes, she got up and left the region of unbelief!

Those people would have been a source of great discouragement to her. Mary left and went to stay with those of "like precious faith" (2 Peter 1:1) - people who could encourage her in her situation, people who knew what it meant to believe and receive a seemingly impossible word from God. That is where many Christians today lose their victory. They have heard the Word of God buy they sit down with ungodly people who scorn the Word. People who say that speaking in tongues is of the devil; healing is not for us today; etc. No wonder they get dragged down to that level of unbelief. Mary left and went to be with the ones who knew and understood what she was going through. You and I today need to also walk with people of like precious faith. That is one of the key reasons why you should always be in church; a good, Bible-believing church.

In the book of Acts chapter 4 the apostles were persecuted for healing the man at the Gate called Beautiful, and for preaching in the name of Jesus. Upon their release from custody, the Bible says that they went back to 'their own company' (Acts 4:23), people who believed like they did. We need to do that too.

Jesus did the same thing. In the book of Mark chapter 5 He was on His way to heal Jairus' daughter when the news arrived that she had already died. Jesus told the crowd that was with Him that they could not come any further. He took only Jairus, Peter, James and John with Him. When they reached Jairus' house, Jesus got rid of all the mourners who had gathered. There are times when you need to either remove yourself from the company of, or get rid of those people who do not favour your faith. If you are going to walk by faith, you need to be in the company of people of like precious faith.

Your faith can either work for you or against you. Instead of using your faith against yourself, why not put it to work for you? You hold the reigns of your life, not Satan. Do not let the enemy intimidate you. It is time to get back all those things that Satan has stolen from you. Find scriptures on which you can base your faith. Then open your mouth and boldly declare that this year is going to be the most glorious year of your life - with more of God, greater victory, bigger blessings, excellent health. A year of increase in every area of your life! Speak it out again.

Chapter Eleven
ARE YOU PASSING YOUR PROSPERITY TEST?

Everything you and I enjoy today is as a result of what Jesus purchased for us at Calvary. The people in the Old Testament got blessed by God because of what Jesus was going to do. We are blessed today because of what Jesus has done.

When we talk about prosperity, it is not just about finances. It also has to do with several other areas of our lives. By 'prosperity' we mean the ability to use God's resources and abilities to meet our needs - spirit, soul, and body. The first prosperity God has promised to man is spiritual - to be born again; to receive Jesus Christ as our Lord and Saviour. Then there is physical prosperity - healing and living in divine health. God has also promised us material and financial prosperity, but as is the case with all His other promises, there are conditions that must be met in order to experience the promised blessings.

There are *prosperity tests* that we must successfully pass in order to receive God's abundant provision in every area of our lives. God's tests however, are not like the devil's.

He does not throw circumstances at us in order to tempt us or to make us fall. God's purpose is to find out if He has first place in your heart; if you will obey Him, even in the face of contradictory or difficult circumstances; if your motives are pure; if you will be faithful with little, so that He can entrust you with more. You must pay the price of obedience to enjoy the blessings of God.

Let us look at some individuals in the Bible and see what their *prosperity tests* involved, and how well they passed them. You will notice how these tests are not necessarily financial in nature, although passing the tests will result in blessings in every area, including material and financial.

Joseph in Egypt

In the book of Genesis we read of Joseph, who was blessed by God in Potiphar's house, and was prospering in all that he did. Potiphar's wife later started propositioning him daily to *lie* with her. Joseph however, refused to yield. That was a test and he passed it, even though in the natural there was nothing to show that he had passed. But payday was coming down the road.

Eventually Joseph was "promoted" from Potiphar's house to prison, after being falsely accused by Mrs. Potiphar of attempted rape. In Potiphar's house, he had learned to manage one person's business well, but in jail God taught him how to manage the affairs of many people. In the eyes of the world Joseph had suffered *demotion*, but in God's eyes it was *promotion*. In prison, Joseph dealt with a cross-section of the Egyptian society. He got to meet some prominent, well connected political prisoners. Once again he faithfully passed this prosperity test, and in time his prospering was apparent to all!

130

Moses qualifies to lead

Moses was in the wilderness, on the backside of the desert where nobody knew him (Exodus 3). He had to serve Jethro the priest of Midian, for forty years. That wasn't what he wanted to do, or what he felt like doing, but he did it faithfully nevertheless. Moses had to learn to take care of the sheep of the man of God, and that qualified him to be able to take care of the sheep of God, the children of Israel.

Israel's wilderness experience

> *"Every commandment which I command you today you must be careful to observe, that you may live and multiply, and go in and possess the land of which the Lord swore to your fathers. And you shall remember that the Lord your God led you all the way these forty years in the wilderness, to humble you and test you, to know what was in your heart, whether you would keep His commandments or not. So He humbled you, allowed you to hunger, and fed you with manna which you did not know nor did your fathers know, that He might make you know that man shall not live by bread alone; but man lives by every word that proceeds from the mouth of the Lord.*
>
> *Deuteronomy 8:1-3*

God never intended to kill the children of Israel in the wilderness on the way from Egypt to the promised land. He was the one who had led them in there. They were meant to pass all the tests they faced, but they failed them with flying colors! Passing or failing, determined who would go into the promised land, and who would die in the wilderness.

There were two ways to get to the promised land and one way was longer than the other. The Bible says that God led the children of Israel through the longer way. This was firstly because they were not trained to fight, and secondly because they had not yet learned God's ways - that was one of the reasons why they had ended up in slavery in Egypt. They had forgotten even the name of their God, and they had to learn His ways afresh.

They were led on their way by a pillar of cloud by day, and a pillar of fire by night - visible manifestations of the glory and presence of God. This is a type of us believers today being led by the Holy Spirit.

Egypt, where the Israelites were in slavery, represented the land of *"not enough"*. The wilderness where God met their physical needs one day at a time, represented the land of *"just enough"*. But Canaan, the promised land, was the land of *"more than enough"*. As we the children of God today, endeavour to prosper in different areas of our lives, we will usually experience a process of moving from the land of *not enough*, through the land of *just enough*, into the land of *more than enough*. The sooner we learn to be led by the Holy Spirit, and walk in obedience to God, the sooner we will live out our days in **the land of more than enough**!

In the book of Exodus chapter 15, the Israelites had just crossed the Red Sea, and for three days they rejoiced and sang praises to God. Then they came to a place where the water was bitter and undrinkable, and they promptly lost their victory, grumbling and complaining against Moses and God.

So many Christians can't keep their victory for more than three days either! Are you grumbling and complaining because you do not have what you need or want? When you act like that you are actually failing your prosperity test, thereby disqualifying yourself from the provision of

God which can only be received by faith. God, who has led you thus far, knows what to do to meet all your needs.

King Solomon asks for wisdom

Shortly after Solomon became king, the Lord appeared to him, and told him to ask for anything and He would do it for him (1 Kings 3:3-15). How would you have responded? This was your chance to ask for anything you could possibly desire in the whole, wide, world!

Solomon asked for wisdom and understanding, which would enable him to serve effectively as king over God's people, and to be a blessing to them. The Lord was so impressed with Solomon's request (he had passed his prosperity test magnificently!), that He gave him riches and honour, and long life as well. God is not short on riches, but there are many He cannot trust with them because they keep failing the prerequisite tests.

Israel returns from captivity

> *In the second year of King Darius, in the sixth month, on the first day of the month, the word of the Lord came by Haggai the prophet to Zerubbabel the son of Shealtiel, governor of Judah, and to Joshua the son of Jehozadak, the high priest, saying, "Thus speaks the Lord of hosts, saying: 'This people says, "The time has not come, the time that the Lord's house should be built."'"*
> *Then the word of the Lord came by Haggai the prophet, saying, "Is it time for you yourselves to dwell in your paneled houses, and this temple[a] to lie in ruins?" Now therefore, thus says the Lord of hosts: "Consider your ways!*
>
> Haggai 1:1-5

Prior to this time, the Israelites had been in captivity in Babylon. It was their sin of forsaking God and serving idols that had caused them to go into captivity in the first place. Now they had been allowed to return to their land, slavery and captivity were over! The time had come for them to start rebuilding their country.

The first thing God wanted them to do was to rebuild His temple. However, as the people began to prosper and own property, instead of putting God first and building His temple, they focused on building their own homes and having a good time. Their actions revealed where their hearts were. He was the one who had delivered them from captivity, and already they were forgetting Him.

About eighteen years earlier, King Cyrus of Babylon had decreed that the temple of the Lord should be built. Eighteen years had now passed and Israel had not done a thing about it. God had given them enough time to get busy with the work, but the temple was still in ruins. Before tending to their own houses, He had expected them to first take care of His house, where He would dwell in their midst.

God's desire has always been to dwell among His people. Even before they reached the promised land, He had them build a tabernacle - a portable tent of worship which they carried with them as they travelled through the wilderness. Now that the Jews had returned to their land from captivity, they knew that for them to effectively worship Him, they had to do it in the temple. Evidently then, they did not have it in their hearts to worship God or put Him first. Things were getting better for them, so they stopped seeking and trusting God.

Consider your ways

"You have sown much, and bring in little; You eat, but do not have enough; You drink, but you are not filled with drink; You clothe yourselves, but no one is warm; And he

who earns wages, Earns wages to put into a bag with holes." Thus says the Lord of hosts: "Consider your ways! Go up to the mountains and bring wood and build the temple, that I may take pleasure in it and be glorified," says the Lord.

Haggai 1:6-8

This can happen to Christians too. No matter how much they make, it is never enough. There is always something waiting to snatch it away. Whenever money comes in, some unexpected expenditure arises and they end up broke again. If you are in a situation like this, then it is time for you to begin to consider *your* ways.

"*Consider your ways*" means, stop and judge yourself. Scrutinize yourself in the presence of God, by His Spirit and by His word. Let the word reveal to you things about yourself that you may not want to see. If you are to make progress, and if you are going to be blessed, you will have to deal with those issues.

Some believers do not really want God, all they want is what He's got. They just want to get close enough to Him to grab His blessings and leave. That kind of half-hearted devotion *seems* to work for a while; suddenly some terrible trouble hits, and then they desperately start seeking God. If this describes you, God is telling you to change, and to consider yours ways!

When problems arise in our lives and things are not happening the way the Bible says they should, we shouldn't just sweep matters under the carpet and hope things will change on their own. If your situation is critical, things have not been working for you, then it is time to change, and in many cases it will require a drastic change.

When people change, they have to make sure that they *stay changed,* and do not go back to the way they used to be. Change is inconvenient and it will take you out of your comfort zone. To make that change you must be willing to pay the price. In Haggai those people had to pay the price - they had to leave all they were doing for themselves to go and build the house of God. Giving priority to the things of God, and putting His temple first, would cost them time and money; their flesh would suffer some inconvenience.

Today we are God's temple - individually and collectively, and it is by doing the work of God that His temple is being built. Many church people think that their pastor is supposed to do all the work. Others feel that if they serve in any area within the church they can do it any old way they want. What they fail to realize is that whatever they do, should be done as unto the Lord, and not unto men, for it is from Him we receive our reward.

For example, you may be called to be an usher in your church. You need to pray before each service. Somebody may come in with a heavy burden, and you go up to them with an anointed handshake and a smile to welcome them in. A miracle could begin to work right there in their lives! Maybe you serve in the children's church or Sunday school. This is not glorified babysitting, it is a vital ministry where precious children are taught to begin to fall in love with Jesus.

There is an anointing to do whatever we do for the Lord, so long as we do it as unto Him, just as if Jesus were right there with us. Right here is a prosperity test which many believers are failing again and again - they are failing in the areas of faithfulness, commitment, and attitude. There is a price to pay for your prosperity, and many without realizing it are failing the tests, especially because they do not see the connection between their obedience in seemingly unrelated issues, and their prosperity.

> Then Haggai answered and said, "'So is this people, and so is this nation before Me,' says the Lord, 'and so is every work of their hands; and what they offer there is unclean.
> 'And now, carefully consider from this day forward: from before stone was laid upon stone in the temple of the Lord - since those days, when one came to a heap of twenty ephahs, there were but ten; when one came to the wine vat to draw out fifty baths from the press, there were but twenty. I struck you with blight and mildew and hail in all the labors of your hands; yet you did not turn to Me,' says the Lord. 'Consider now from this day forward, from the twenty-fourth day of the ninth month, from the day that the foundation of the Lord's temple was laid—consider it: Is the seed still in the barn? As yet the vine, the fig tree, the pomegranate, and the olive tree have not yielded fruit. But from this day I will bless you.'"
>
> *Haggai 2:14-19*

From the very day that the Israelites laid the foundation of the temple, the moment they began to change their ways, God began to bless them. He restored unto them all they had lost, and more! God promised to do this in the very same year. All the people had to do was begin to obey God and set their hearts toward His instructions, and He began to open the heavens and pour out the rains. They had now passed their prosperity test.

The Macedonian churches

In 2 Corinthians 8:2, Paul testified of the churches in Macedonia;

> Out of the most severe trial, their overflowing joy and their extreme poverty welled up in rich generosity.
>
> *2 Corinthians 8:2 (NIV)*

In their deep poverty they were still giving generously to the church, and they did it joyfully too! That was a test.

When many Christians do not have enough, they become grumpy and sad, and say, "this prosperity stuff doesn't work!" They fail to realize that they have just failed their prosperity test, and now God cannot trust them with greater blessings.

When Joseph was suddenly promoted to Prime Minister of Egypt, he did not have to learn to do the job, he knew how to do it already. When he became powerful he did not go after Potiphar's wife, or try to get even with his wicked brothers who had sold him into slavery. He was not vengeful or vindictive. Joseph's right attitude determined the altitude to which he rose. It qualified him for divine promotion.

Have you been failing key tests in your life? God hasn't been able to promote you and prosper you as He has desired. Maybe you have been unfaithful, disobedient, ungrateful and impatient; other things have taken priority over God in your life. Maybe your attitude has been wrong. Well, consider your ways, give careful thought to your ways and judge yourself. Failure in these other areas of your life will hinder you from realizing the fullness of God's blessings. If you have been failing your prosperity tests, God is so merciful that He will let you take them again. This time, pass them with honours in Jesus' name!

Chapter Twelve
PRAISE: THE WAY TO MORE THAN ENOUGH

Could you do with extra vitality, health and energy? Could you do with more wisdom, material resources and finances? If you're like me, I am sure you can! The Bible teaches us the sure way to have more than enough of all that God has provided for us in Christ.

In the book of Joshua chapter 18, seven of the twelve tribes of Israel had not even begun to inherit what God had given to them - the land flowing with milk and honey. The tribe of Judah had received their portion of the inheritance, and it was too much for them. They took everything in sight and beyond, and Judah at this time was not even one of the big tribes!

> *The inheritance of the Simeonites was taken from the share of Judah, because Judah's portion was more than they needed. So the Simeonites received their inheritance within the territory of Judah.*
>
> *Joshua 19:9*

This is a type of the church today. Jesus our Messiah, the head of the church, came from the tribe of Judah, and we like Judah are supposed to have more than enough.

Judah had more land than they needed, so they asked the children of the tribe of Simeon, "Have you taken your inheritance yet? No? Then you just take that whole portion of our land and we won't even know you are there. Take as much as you want." That's the way it should be with us today in the body of Christ. We should have more than we need, with enough left over to bless those who don't have.

Simeon is figurative of those who are downtrodden and beaten down. Simeon's tribe had not been able to claim its own portion of the inheritance. Thank God Judah had more than enough and he could give Simeon as much as he wanted. "Judah" means praise; in other words, with praise in our hearts and on our lips, we too can have more than enough! Alleluia!

Journey from "Praise" to "Sin"

> *Now it came to pass, in the days when the judges ruled, that there was a famine in the land. And a certain man of Bethlehem, Judah, went to dwell in the country of Moab, he and his wife and his two sons.*
>
> *Ruth 1:1*

Bethlehem is in Judah where Jesus was born. "Judah" we said means praise. "Moab" denotes sin, and is actually a type of the backslidden world. So this man uprooted his family, he took his wife and his two sons, and left "praise" to sojourn, or to go temporarily, into "sin".

> *The name of the man was Elimelech, the name of his wife was Naomi, and the names of his two sons were Mahlon and*

Chilion—Ephrathites of Bethlehem, Judah. And they went to the country of Moab and remained there. Then Elimelech, Naomi's husband, died; and she was left, and her two sons. Now they took wives of the women of Moab: the name of the one was Orpah, and the name of the other Ruth. And they dwelt there about ten years.

Ruth 1: 2-4

They left the house of praise because of famine and went temporarily into "sin" to find relief. But instead of the quick trip they had planned, they ended up staying there for ten years, only for the man and his two sons to eventually die. That is what can happen to you when you decide to "temporarily" step outside of God into sin! By the time they were coming back, three of them were dead, they had died in sin!

You do not want to leave "praise" for anything. You do not want to leave the place God has planted you in, or the presence of God for anything; not temporarily, not for any portion of time! If you do, it may cost you more than what you bargained for. If Elimelech's family had chosen to stay in "praise" (Judah), no doubt God would have ensured that they had more than enough to meet their needs.

A nation seeks the Lord

In the book of 2 Chronicles chapter 20 we read of the little country of Judah. They were following God, and Jehoshaphat the king served God as best as he knew how. Then he was given the bad news that three armies had banded together and were coming against him. One of those armies alone was enough to take care of Judah militarily, not to talk of three! There was no United Nations Organization back then, so when enemies came against you, that was it. So what did Jehoshaphat do?

> *And Jehoshaphat feared, and set himself to seek the Lord, and proclaimed a fast throughout all Judah.*
>
> 2 Chronicles 20:3

He did not take off and go to Moab, or try to compromise and make peace with his enemies. He chose to seek the Lord.

When hard times hit, when it seems like your whole world is caving in on you, what are you going to do? Are you going to jump up and start making phone calls all over town, or are you going to do what the Bible tells you to do and seek the Lord?

God was not surprised by the armies that attacked Jehoshaphat, He knew about it beforehand. God knows what He is going to do not only about the problems you have now, but also about the ones you are yet to face! But you will have to seek Him for His solutions. Most of the time when pressures come against us, we start calling people; we want to borrow money; we look to men for help, but none of these things help.

> *So Judah gathered together to ask help from the Lord; and from all the cities of Judah they came to seek the Lord.*
> *Then Jehoshaphat stood in the assembly of Judah and Jerusalem, in the house of the Lord, before the new court, and said: "O Lord God of our fathers, are You not God in heaven, and do You not rule over all the kingdoms of the nations, and in Your hand is there not power and might, so that no one is able to withstand You? Are You not our God, who drove out the inhabitants of this land before Your people Israel, and gave it to the descendants of Abraham Your friend forever? And they dwell in it, and have built You a sanctuary in it for Your name, saying, 'If disaster comes upon us - sword, judgment, pestilence, or famine - we will stand before this temple and in Your presence (for Your name is in this temple), and cry out to You in our affliction, and You will hear and save.'*
>
> 2 Chronicles 20:4-9

See how Jehoshaphat is praying here. He brings the word of God, His covenant, before Him. "Lord, this is what You said when this house was built, this is why you had this house built; for Your presence and Your name to be in this place, so that when we stand before this place and pray concerning anything, You said You would hear and help with certainty. No "ifs", "buts", or "maybes", You will hear and You will help"!

Knowledge of God's word is what gives us confidence in prayer. We need to take the word of God with us when we go to pray. The book of Psalms chapter 91 says;

> *He shall call upon Me, and I will answer him; I will be with him in trouble; I will deliver him and honor him.*
>
> *Psalm 91:15*

Scriptures like this will give you confidence when you pray in your day of trouble. Lillian B. Yeomans made this statement: ***"Faith is being able to step onto the aching void with nothing but the word of God underneath your feet."***

Do not wait until you are backed into a corner before you seek God and hold onto His word. Seek Him even when everything seems to be going fine, that way you will get good at it, and know what to do in the day of trouble.

Make your problem God's problem

King Jehoshaphat comes before God in 2 Chronicles 20:10-12 and says in effect, "If it were not for You who prevented us Lord, we would have destroyed these people on our way here from Egypt, and then they wouldn't have been here to attack us today. Now see how they reward us, by coming to throw us out of Your possession which You gave us to inherit!" Here Jehoshaphat makes his problem

God's problem. Jehoshaphat is saying that he and God are one; they are in covenant together. If Judah is in trouble, then it is also God's trouble; the enemies had come to cast them out of God's possession.

You might say, "God knows what I am going through. Why doesn't He just go ahead and help me?" Jesus told us that even though God knows what your request is before you pray, you still have to go ahead and ask. Yes, God knows everything, but we still have to give Him the legal right to intervene in our circumstances - He doesn't just butt in uninvited. He wants to help us, but how many people are inviting Him in? Most people are trying to fix things on their own, and tell God to take a back seat and watch them solve their problems themselves. Oh, how it breaks His heart to see the mess we make of our lives over and over again!

Believe and receive the Word of God

The word of the Lord came to Jahaziel the prophet and he declares to the king and all Judah,

> And he said, "Listen, all you of Judah and you inhabitants of Jerusalem, and you, King Jehoshaphat! Thus says the Lord to you: 'Do not be afraid nor dismayed because of this great multitude, for the battle is not yours, but God's. Tomorrow go down against them. They will surely come up by the Ascent of Ziz, and you will find them at the end of the brook before the Wilderness of Jeruel. You will not need to fight in this battle. Position yourselves, stand still and see the salvation of the Lord, who is with you, O Judah and Jerusalem!' Do not fear or be dismayed; tomorrow go out against them, for the Lord is with you."
>
> *2 Chronicles 20:15-17*

When the children of Israel were at the edge of the Red Sea, God said the same thing, "Fear not, stand still, and see the salvation of the Lord." You have to see yourself delivered before your deliverance manifests; you have to see the bills paid before they get paid; you have to see yourself healed before it happens.

In hundreds of places the Bible exhorts us to "fear not", to "not be dismayed, neither be discouraged" Nowhere are we told to be full of fear, to be scared, sad or mad! It is very easy to be discouraged, all you have to do is look around you, and see and hear what is going on in the world. We do not look at those things, we look to God for our salvation and provision.

When I was a kid, there were bullies in the neighbourhood, and like everyone else, I was scared of them. But whenever I was walking with my parents, I could walk straight up to any bully and talk to him anyway I wanted. Where did I get that boldness from all of a sudden? I had my parents with me, of course. In just the same way, God has said that He is with us, He is in us, and He is for us - all three at the same time! Anyway you want to look at it, we have it made! Go out against the circumstances, walk right up in the devil's face and tell him to wait and see the miracle Jesus is going to do for you today! That is how we should walk and talk. Why? Because we believe what God has said.

The sure weapon of praise

And Jehoshaphat bowed his head with his face to the ground, and all Judah and the inhabitants of Jerusalem bowed before the Lord, worshiping the Lord. Then the Levites of the children of the Kohathites and of the children of the Korahites stood up to praise the Lord God of Israel with voices loud and high.

2 Chronicles 20:18-19,

We all love to enjoy a good ball game every now and then. Take for example football's Super Bowl night. All of North America gathers to watch the game, cheer and get all excited. At the end of the game, are their bills paid? Are their emotional problems solved? Are their families united and blessed? No. I am not saying watching sports is a bad thing, but if we cannot shout about the greatness of our God, and if we cannot shout about what God has done for us in Jesus, then we have no business shouting about anything else in this life. People pay good money to watch a game and shout in support of people they do not even know. But when it comes to shouting about the God who is King of kings and Lord of lords, they complain that we are too loud.

The Bible says these people praised the Lord with a loud voice. They must have believed what the prophet of God said to them. They hadn't even gone into battle yet, and they were already praising the Lord, shouting, rejoicing, singing. What a people! If we cannot shout, sing and dance about the truth of God's word, and what He has done for us, we have got no business shouting about anything. When you praise and shout and sing and dance about the Lord, you are going to see results in your personal life. It is going to positively affect your body, your mind, your family, and your finances.

> *And when he had consulted with the people, he appointed those who should sing to the Lord, and who should praise the beauty of holiness, as they went out before the army and were saying: "Praise the Lord, For His mercy endures forever."*
>
> 2 Chronicles 20:21

Instead of putting the generals in front of the army, King Jehoshaphat put a big choir in front of them to sing! Who ever heard of going to war like that? God loves to do things in unusual ways, just so He alone will get the glory! How would you have liked to be one of the members of that choir, singing out to meet three enemy armies? That is the way we need to face those enemies today - the enemies of sin, sickness, lack, oppression, depression and bondage.

> *Now when they began to sing and to praise, the Lord set ambushes against the people of Ammon, Moab, and Mount Seir, who had come against Judah; and they were defeated.*
>
> 2 Chronicles 20:22

When did their answer come? Was it when they were praying, or while they were praising? It was while they were praising.

God is showing us something here. In the book of Acts chapter 16, Paul and Silas prayed and sang praises to God, and the prisoners heard them. When did the answer to the problem they were facing come? Was it when they were praying, or while they were praising? While they were praising. Often times we pray, but how about praying and praising? Praise is the highest kind of prayer.

The Lord once spoke to me and said, "If people will spend at least thirty minutes a day praising and ministering to me, having their focus on me instead of their problems, then they will see those problems of long continuance (or long standing) which they have had, all wiped out and replaced with blessings. Many people have prayed and prayed. They have prayed it backwards, forwards, sideways, they have prayed it in every way they can, all to no avail. Well it is now time to pray and praise!

The spoils of praise

> *For the people of Ammon and Moab stood up against the inhabitants of Mount Seir to utterly kill and destroy them. And when they had made an end of the inhabitants of Seir, they helped to destroy one another.*
> *So when Judah came to a place overlooking the wilderness, they looked toward the multitude; and there were their dead bodies, fallen on the earth. No one had escaped.*
>
> *2 Chronicles 20:23-24*

They killed each other. Judah did not have to unsheathe a sword to fight that day. Think about that; the last two guys had to kill each other simultaneously. These countries lost their armies that day, with no casualties on Judah's side. What a way to win a battle. When the Lord fights for you, He does it in style! You may not know how He is going to do it, but He will.

> *When Jehoshaphat and his people came to take away their spoil, they found among them an abundance of valuables on the dead bodies,[a] and precious jewelry, which they stripped off for themselves, more than they could carry away; and they were three days gathering the spoil because there was so much.*
>
> *2 Chronicles 20:25*

In other words, when the Lord told Judah to go out against the armies, what He actually had in mind was not for them to fight, but for them to go out and gather the spoil - more than they could carry! Praise had released the power of God for victory, and His superabundant blessings!

Jehoshaphat said, "Our eyes are upon Thee." Their eyes were not upon the enemy, they were not upon the problem, neither were they on man to come and help them. Their eyes were on God. When we praise God, our eyes are on Him and we see our salvation in Him. We see Him healing our bodies, taking care of our families, giving us wisdom to tackle our problems. We see all these things with our inner eyes, the eyes of faith. It takes faith to follow God.

We were made to praise God, no day should pass without you giving glory to the Lord and thanking Him. A lifestyle of praise like this will bring a release of God's increase, blessing you, and causing you to be a blessing to many others.

According to Judges 5:11, we should be among those who *"recount the righteous acts of the Lord..."* Praise God for your many blessings; the food you eat, your health, your job, your family and children, and all the wonderful things you have. You and I just don't know how many accidents, injuries and devastating circumstances, God has delivered us from on this side of heaven. But there are some things that we do know, and we should bring them up again and again, recounting them and thanking Him. Praise Him everyday. Praise the Lord today!

Chapter Thirteen
NO MORE CONDEMNATION

Have you ever been in a situation where you wanted to do the right thing, but somehow ended up doing wrong? Everyone has. Many Christians, in an attempt to understand their struggle with sin, have turned to the book of Romans chapter 7 as an explanation for their moral dilemma;

> *But now, it is no longer I who do it, but sin that dwells in me. For I know that in me (that is, in my flesh) nothing good dwells; for to will is present with me, but how to perform what is good I do not find. For the good that I will to do, I do not do; but the evil I will not to do, that I practice. Now if I do what I will not to do, it is no longer I who do it, but sin that dwells in me.*
> *I find then a law, that evil is present with me, the one who wills to do good. For I delight in the law of God according to the inward man. But I see another law in my members, warring against the law of my mind, and bringing me into captivity to the law of sin which is in my members. O wretched man that I am! Who will deliver me from this body of death?*
>
> *Romans 7:17-24*

There is a problem however with the conclusion that this passage is describing the Christian experience. The person being described here by Paul (the writer of the book of Romans) does not sound anything like a new creation in Christ. That is why it is so important to continue to read on to Romans chapter 8;

> *There is therefore now no condemnation to those who are in Christ Jesus, who do not walk according to the flesh, but according to the Spirit. For the law of the Spirit of life in Christ Jesus has made me free from the law of sin and death.*
>
> Romans 8:1-2

"*There is therefore* **NOW** *no condemnation*" clearly shows us that what Paul had previously been talking about in the preceding verses of Romans chapter 7, does not apply to those who are **NOW** in Christ Jesus. This is why the Bible instructs us to study to show ourselves approved unto God so that we can rightly divide the word of truth (2 Timothy 2:15). If the Word of God can be rightly divided, then by implication, it can also be wrongly divided.

In the book of Romans chapter 7 Paul describes his dilemma as a Jew, trying to live right before God under the old covenant and the law. The law however, was not designed for man to keep it. In actual fact God designed it to reveal the fallen spiritual state of man, in order that man could see himself in his true condition - hopeless and helpless without God and in desperate need of a saviour. That is why Jesus Christ came to fulfill the righteousness requirements of the law on our behalf, so that His righteousness could then be credited to us! Glory to God!

In Christ

I was raised in a religious family. We did not just go to church every Sunday, we got there early and left there late! At age 12 or 13, I remember wondering about what I needed to do to secure a place in Heaven. After talking to different people, I eventually concluded that if my good deeds outweighed my bad deeds, then I would make it to heaven. One day I set out to actually record everything I did that day under two columns, good and bad. I put a check mark in the good column for every good thing I did, and a check mark in the bad column for every wrong thing I did. Unfortunately for me, before the day was out, I had gotten into two fights, my school uniform got ripped, etc. Needless to say, my bad deeds outweighed my good deeds that day and I felt so miserable!

My condition was exactly like that of Paul in Romans chapter 7. The harder I tried, the deeper I sank into sin. Praise God however, for the good news in Romans chapter 8. There is now no condemnation for those who are in Christ Jesus! All Paul had to do, all I had to do and all anyone else has to do, is to receive God's free gift of salvation in Christ. Furthermore, the book of 2 Corinthians chapter 5:17 tells us that

> *Therefore, if anyone is in Christ, he is a new creation; old things have passed away; behold, all things have become new.*
>
> *2 Corinthians 5:17*

The old sinner is dead and gone, and a newly recreated person, with the nature of God, has been born.

God sees us only in Christ and that is the way He relates to us. He sees us in Christ and He sees Christ in us. The word 'Christ' is not Jesus' last name, it means 'the Anointed One'. That means that Jesus was anointed by God to be anything you need Him to be. Be it your saviour, healer, deliverer, provider, etc. He is everything you need Him to be to you. The totality of all of God's abundance and all of His resources is stored in this huge depository called 'Christ'. You may find it hard to completely grasp all the implications of this awesome truth, but that is why we simply believe it and accept it by faith.

The Flesh vs The Spirit

There is now no condemnation to those who are in Christ Jesus, but only to those who do not walk (or live) according to the flesh, but according to the Spirit. This means that even as a Christian you have the choice to either live according to your flesh (that is your senses and feelings), or according to the leading of the Spirit of God, who lives inside your human spirit.

Man is made up of three parts: he is a spirit, he has a soul and he lives in a body. It is your spirit that is recreated in Christ at salvation, not your body or flesh. That is why it is possible for your flesh to want to do sinful things, and for your spirit to not want to do them. The book of Hebrews chapter 4 says;

> *For the word of God is living and powerful, and sharper than any two-edged sword, piercing even to the division of soul and spirit, and of joints and marrow, and is a discerner of the thoughts and intents of the heart.*
>
> *Hebrews 4:12*

This reveals that the Word of God is powerful enough to go down into your heart (or spirit), rise up from in you and begin to cleanse your mind (or soul), and even affect your body.

If the enemy can get you to live according to the flesh and thereby bring you under condemnation, then he can paralyze your faith and render you ineffective. Most Christians I know are not looking for ways to sin and get away with it. We are not looking for a way to get as close as possible and still be saved. We want to stay far away from sin.

Now the book of Galatians chapter 5 is very enlightening to our understanding in this area.

> *I say then: Walk in the Spirit, and you shall not fulfill the lust of the flesh. For the flesh lusts against the Spirit, and the Spirit against the flesh; and these are contrary to one another, so that you do not do the things that you wish.*
>
> *Galatians 5:16-17*

The Holy Spirit is teaching us here to live in victory. Most Christians are trying to live the victorious life by trying not to sin. By trying hard not to do the wrong things, they hope they will somehow end up doing the right thing.

Two separate realms exist: the realm of the flesh and the realm of the spirit. If you are walking in one, you cannot be walk in the other. The key to a victorious life is not trying to stay away from walking in the flesh, in the hope that somehow or the other you will wind up walking in the Spirit. Just as you have natural promptings for things like food and rest, likewise you also have spiritual promptings. Learn to recognize and yield to those promptings. For example, you may feel a need to get more into the Word of God, or to spend some time praying in the Holy Spirit. Endeavour to become more sensitive to the Spirit and obey His leadings promptly. Continually feed your human spirit in order to strengthen it, for if you starve your spirit, its voice will grow weaker and weaker, and harder to discern.

Some Christians have felt spiritually hungry, with a prompting to take time out to pray and feed on the word, but instead they respond by eating more physical food! Unfortunately, that is about the only kind of response they know. Whenever you feel God drawing your attention to an area of your life, make sure you deal with it promptly. Otherwise, somebody else may be used to bring it to your attention; the very area in which the Spirit has been dealing with you. Do not get offended at them when this happens, just take the correction and move on.

The choice is yours

When you walk in the Spirit you are starving the lust of the flesh, but if you yield yourself to the desires of the flesh, you will be starving your spirit. The two are contrary to one another.

For example, before you got saved, you might have hung out in the bars every Friday night. Now that you are saved, the real you inside, your spirit, that has been recreated in the image of God, doesn't want to do that anymore. But your flesh, which is not born again, wants to keep on doing what it has always done. At times, your flesh will throw a tantrum, just like a toddler demanding to have its own way. No doubt, resisting the desires of the flesh will be painful sometimes but it is necessary if you want to live free of condemnation.

The Holy Spirit in you will never lead you to do anything that is wrong. The devil however, loves to hear people blame him for their actions - "The devil made me do it." The fact is, if you crucify your flesh, there is nothing the devil has to work with. He can't make you do anything. He can give you a suggestion. He can pressure you, but in the final analysis you have to be the one to say yes or no to him. You have to let your flesh know that now that you are born in again, it has a new boss - your reborn spirit!

Just because I pastor a church does not mean I feel like going to church all the time, anymore than you feel like going to work all the time. My flesh and your flesh will give us every reason under the sun why we shouldn't do what we know we are supposed to do. Though my flesh, with the devil's help, may be screaming at me, I still have the final say. I can choose to say yes or no. Saying no to the flesh is never pleasant or easy, but once I have said no and I choose to act accordingly, the bad feelings eventually leave and the good feelings from the spirit come up. Conversely, when you say yes to the flesh you feel good temporarily, but in the end feelings of condemnation, guilt, shame and regret, are the end result.

The works of the flesh

Now the works of the flesh are evident, which are: adultery,[a] fornication, uncleanness, lewdness, idolatry, sorcery, hatred, contentions, jealousies, outbursts of wrath, selfish ambitions, dissensions, heresies, envy, murders,[b] drunkenness, revelries, and the like; of which I tell you beforehand, just as I also told you in time past, that those who practice such things will not inherit the kingdom of God.

Galatians 5:19-21

In other words, if you yield to the flesh, the flesh will lead you into any or all of the above.

There is something to note about the flesh. After it has led you into something, after a while a little bit of it will no longer be satisfying. That is how people get hooked on things like pornography, drugs, or alcohol. Nobody ever sets out to become an alcoholic. They never say,

"I am going to become an alcoholic today." They start out confidently, claiming to know exactly where their limit is only to find out after it is too late, that they have gone down the road of no return and they are in serious trouble!

It is important to remember that Galatians chapter 5 was written to Christians, not unbelievers. In other words, even though you are a Christian who loves God and you have the Spirit of God in you, it is possible to yield yourself to the lusts of the flesh.

Idolatry is a work of the flesh and many Christians have idols. Their idol might not be an image made out of wood, plastic, or metal. It could be their possessions, wealth, career or a loved one; anything that has a higher priority in their life than God does, and to which they devote their attention. The Bible tells us that God is a jealous God, and He wants our undivided attention.

Do you know that your attitude towards money reveals your attitude towards God? To put it in another way, your attitude towards money and everything money can buy reveals your attitude towards God. The Bible says in the book of 1 John chapter 2,

> *Do not love the world or the things in the world. If anyone loves the world, the love of the Father is not in him.*
>
> *1 John 2:15*

Also the book of Matthew chapter 6 tells us that;

> *"No one can serve two masters; for either he will hate the one and love the other, or else he will be loyal to the one and despise the other. You cannot serve God and mammon (riches).*
>
> *Matthew 6:24*

You cannot serve both God and money. If money is your idol and you love money and the things it can buy, then that simply means that you do not love God.

The fruit of the Spirit

Galatians 5:21 warns of the consequences of yielding to the flesh. Those who produce the works of the flesh will not inherit the kingdom of God. Not inheriting the kingdom of God implies not enjoying the blessings of the kingdom. Praise God however, reading further along brings us to the good news of the fruit of the Spirit.

> *But the fruit of the Spirit is love, joy, peace, longsuffering, kindness, goodness, faithfulness, gentleness, self-control. Against such there is no law.*
>
> *Galatians 5:22-23*

In Galatians 5:19, the works of the flesh are plural, but the fruit of the Spirit is singular. By this the Bible is telling us that the fruit is a cluster, and love will lead you into all the other fruit. Love, being the first fruit that you should show after salvation, is also the parent fruit that will lead to the development of all the other fruit of the Spirit.

The law of the Spirit of life in Christ

What does it mean, when the scripture says in Galatians 5:23, that "against such (the fruit of the Spirit) there is no law"? To answer this we need to take another look at Romans chapter 8;

> *There is therefore now no condemnation to those who are in Christ Jesus, who do not walk according to the flesh, but according to the Spirit. For the law of the Spirit of life in Christ Jesus has made me free from the law of sin and death.*
>
> *Romans 8:1-2*

No longer do we have to be subject to the law of sin and death and all its consequences.

In order to understand this better, picture a truck and a cargo airplane. We all know that a truck cannot fly. Supposing however, you drove the truck into that aircraft, it could take off and fly with the truck on board. Obviously the law of gravity affects everything on this planet including the plane and the truck. The plane however, has been designed in such a way that it is able to engage a law other than the law of gravity, the law of lift. The fact that the plane flies does not mean that the law of gravity has stopped acting on it. The law of gravity continues its operation, but the plane has simply engaged a higher law, the law of lift, which supersedes the effect of gravity.

This law of lift perfectly illustrates what the law of the Spirit of life in Christ can do for us. Just as the truck can stay in the sky because it is inside the plane, likewise, those who are in Christ Jesus, can rise above the law of sin and death. The law of sin and death is still in operation, but those who are in Christ can engage a higher law, the law of the Spirit of life, and rise above the law of sin and death. We can engage that law and free ourselves from the effects of the law of sin and death which reigns here on earth, by walking in the Spirit. Daily we can choose to obey the Word of God and choose to yield to the promptings of the Holy Spirit who lives in us, rather than yield to the desires of our flesh. That is why the Bible tells us to crucify the flesh.

And so we see that Galatians 5:23 is saying that nothing can succeed against the person who walks in the Spirit and produces the fruit of the Spirit. There is no greater law than the law of the Spirit of life in Christ. Nothing can come against the fruit of love, joy, peace, etc., and render it ineffective. And love can never fail.

Condemnation will rob you of confidence

> *My little children, let us not love in word or in tongue, but in deed and in truth. And by this we know[a] that we are of the truth, and shall assure our hearts before Him. For if our heart condemns us, God is greater than our heart, and knows all things.*
>
> 1 John 3:18-20

The Holy Spirit never condemns you when you sin or make a mistake. It is your own spirit, your heart that condemns you. Deep down in you, the Holy Spirit is trying to encourage you and let you know that you are forgiven so that you can move on.

Reading on in the book of 1 John chapter 3, we find that our source of confidence before God is the fact that He does not condemn us;

> *Beloved, if our heart does not condemn us, we have confidence toward God. And whatever we ask we receive from Him, because we keep His commandments and do those things that are pleasing in His sight.*
>
> 1 John 3:21-22

Doing those things that are pleasing in His sight enables us to ask and receive confidence from God.

Satan is a thief and one of the things he comes to steal and destroy is our confidence. That is how he defeats many Christians, by robbing them of their confidence with feelings of condemnation. Many prayers have been rendered ineffective as believers have lost their confidence in prayer. The devil whispers in their ears, "What makes you think God is going to answer your prayer, after all the bad things you have done? You are such a lousy

Christian." The truth is that even without Satan's input, it is part of man's fallen nature to beat himself down.

Condemnation will age you, weigh you down in misery, and even make you sick. It will cause you to lose your confidence before God and hinder your prayers. Regardless of how many times you have failed, how many times you have blown it, the blood of Jesus is powerful enough to cleanse you from all sin. His blood will not only cleanse you from sin, but from the consciousness of sin and also free you from all condemnation. Hallelujah! No more condemnation for you and no more condemnation for me! No more Condemnation for anyone in Christ Jesus who chooses to walk after the Spirit, and not after the flesh. The choice is yours.

Chapter Fourteen
RUN YOUR RACE

Therefore we also, since we are surrounded by so great a cloud of witnesses, let us lay aside every weight, and the sin which so easily ensnares us, and let us run with endurance the race that is set before us, looking unto Jesus, the author and finisher of our faith, who for the joy that was set before Him endured the cross, despising the shame, and has sat down at the right hand of the throne of God.

Hebrews 12:1-2

God has called every believer to run a spiritual race. In this passage, the Christian's spiritual race is likened to that of an athlete. You have yours to run, and I have mine. However, this is not a hundred-meter dash, it is a marathon.

Hebrews 12:1 above mentions a "cloud of witnesses". Who are they? They are those members of the body of Christ who are no longer here on earth, but have gone on to Heaven. They are spectators in the grandstands, watching us run our spiritual race and urging us on. They are not interested in natural things, or in aspects of our daily life, like what dress or house we just bought. They are only interested in the spiritual progress that you and I are making. The Bible tells us that angels in Heaven rejoice over even one sinner that repents, and these witnesses are rejoicing right along with them! If you are not saved yet, then you haven't even approached the starting line. To receive the winner's prize, the athlete has to finish the race and run according to the rules. This is also true spiritually. Let us look at some of those rules.

Rule 1: Lay aside the weights
In every race there are rules. The Bible gives us the rules for our race, the instructions on how to run it. First, Hebrews 12:1 tells us that we must lay aside every weight. Unlike the Old Testament saints, we New Testament believers have the Holy Spirit in us. One of the reasons why we have the Holy Spirit inside us is so that we can know what the weights are that we need to lay aside. When the Spirit is dealing with you about which weights to lay aside, He is talking specifically to you. Do not go and tell somebody else to lay aside the very same weights.

A good illustration is that of a married couple who testified that when they got married they felt the Lord telling them not to own a television for the first two years of their marriage. Did that mean that owning a television was bad? No, but it can be a weight if you watch too much of it. The couple said it was hard at first, but after two years they didn't feel like going back to owning a television, and they ended up not owning one for four years! They said they would not trade those four years for anything, for they got to know each other very well. Now they do have a television, but it has its place. It does not take precedence over the more important things in their lives.

Some people do not even realize they have a problem in this area. Someone once told me that when it was too cold outside, instead of going to church they just stayed home and watched church services on television. But who does he call when he is in trouble, the TV preacher? No. He calls his local pastor! Somebody else said that their home was really blessed and full of the glory of God because their television was tuned to Christian channels and on 24 hours a day! That doesn't mean they are spiritual. Not everything on Christian television is godly, and the devil gets on Christian television too! I am not against Christian television, but we must be balanced in everything we do.

In order to fully understand what it means to lay aside weights, just imagine that today you were to run a race in the Olympics. You would have to dress appropriately in order to stand any chance of winning. For example, Donovan Bailey, the Canadian one hundred-metre Olympic champion in 1996, once ran a race in which he wore running shoes that weighed only four ounces! Bailey did not want anything to weigh him down in his pursuit of glory; he laid aside every weight!

Read the story of Lazarus in the book of John chapter 11 and you will notice that when Jesus raised Lazarus from the dead and he came out of the tomb, Jesus did not allow him to go into town the way he was. Lazarus was wrapped up in grave clothes, strips of cloth that had been wrapped around his entire body with special ointments for the purpose of embalming him. Jesus said, *"Loose him, and let him go."* (John 11:44). Today, there are many who have been raised from the dead in Christ (that is, they are born again), but they are still bound and weighed down by their grave clothes. You cannot run your spiritual race in grave clothes; they are not designed for running! In order to run our race effectively, we each need to get rid of our own "grave clothes" – the things we have carried over from the way we used to live when we were spiritually dead (before we got saved). I'm talking about the wrong and negative ways in which we used to think, speak, and act. It is these fleshly things that weigh Christians down.

Rule 2: Lay aside the sin

Notice that the scripture says that we are to lay aside "every weight, *and the sin...*" There are many things that could be "weights" that are not necessarily "sins". Watching television is not a sin in itself, although there are things on the it that are sinful. You have to be able to judge things for yourself. Is it hindering you or is it a boost to you in the race that you are running today?

We have not been called to live a life of do's and don'ts. Some Christians just go around asking whether or not it is right to do this or that. In some of these areas, where the issue at hand is not an outright sin, only you can tell. Ask yourself some key questions. Is it giving glory to the Lord? Will it bring me closer to God? That is why the Bible says we should lay aside every weight, and the sin, which does so easily beset us. If you learn to deal with the weights, the sin will not be a problem. There is no particular sin that goes by the name "besetting sin", but every sin has the potential to beset, or persistently harass you. What you do with it is the same thing you do with all other sins. You repent of it, and receive God's grace to forsake it.

Rule 3: Preparation time is never wasted time

In the book of Acts chapter 13, we find certain prophets and teachers in the church at Antioch getting together to pray.

> As they ministered to the Lord and fasted, the Holy Spirit said, "Now separate to Me Barnabas and Saul for the work to which I have called them."
>
> Acts 13:2

Paul and Barnabas were already in the ministry at this time. Paul was a prophet and teacher, and Barnabas was a teacher. Though they were doing the work of the ministry, they had not even begun to fulfill the ultimate call that God had for them. Up to this point in time, all they had been doing was preparing themselves to fill that place of ministry that God wanted them in.

Naturally speaking there are people today who are doctors, teachers, and other kinds of professionals. None of them started to practice their profession without first undergoing years of preparation and training. A teacher for instance, spends many years studying, being trained, and practicing under someone else's guidance. Spiritually speaking it is the same. You are not going to start where God ultimately wants to use you. None of us will. You will find that when you first start your spiritual journey with God, He will use you in almost any area of ministry. Your heart is going to be proved and tested repeatedly in different situations. You are going to meet all kinds of people; some of whom will treat you right, and others who will treat you wrong. All that is designed to prove or test you, to find out if you are going to run your race to the end and win.

There are all kinds of stories behind the victories of Olympic athletes. Some of them tell of athletes whose countries started training them sixteen years before their event. When you are being prepared like that there are some things that you will just have to do without. For example, Mohammed Ali trained and became the world's greatest boxer. He had this vision burning so deeply in his heart that he would train everyday, regardless of circumstances. As a schoolboy, instead of riding the bus to school, he would jog there and back. His classmates would pass him in the bus, laugh at him, and throw things at him. But his burning desire spurred him on, for he believed he was called to box and was willing to prepare himself in whatever way necessary to fulfill his dream. How can we who are racing for eternal rewards do any less?

Rule 4: No pain, no gain

Do you not know that those who run in a race all run, but one receives the prize? Run in such a way that you may obtain it. And everyone who competes for the prize is temperate in all things. Now they do it to obtain a perishable crown, but we for an imperishable crown. Therefore I run thus: not with uncertainty. Thus I fight: not as one who beats the air. But I discipline my body and bring it into subjection, lest, when I have preached to others, I myself should become disqualified.

1 Corinthians 9:24-27

Paul tells us here, that in natural things people go through such severe discipline. They torture themselves so that they may win a temporary, perishable prize. Great athletes deny themselves of the many worldly pleasures that their friends pursue, because of the goals they are striving to realize in their lives. Today, Mohammed Ali is better known than most of his peers. He paid the price!

There is a price to pay for anything in life that is going to bring you to a place of recognition, or a place of blessing.

Hebrews 12:2 states that Jesus is the example we are to follow. We are not to follow His example by dying on the cross like He did. In that situation He was our substitute. We are to follow His example in the way that He was willing to endure suffering and pain, for the glory that He knew was beyond the cross. Likewise, God wants us to run our race with endurance and be willing to discipline ourselves so that we can enjoy our full inheritance in Christ, here on earth and in the life to come.

Rule 5: Get your priorities straight

Someone once said that he thought getting up to read his Bible and pray everyday was mechanical and religious. Accordingly, he only read and prayed when he felt the Spirit moving him to. My response to that was to ask why he didn't eat or bathe only when he felt the Spirit? Why didn't he go to work only when he felt the Spirit? People do not act that way with natural things because they know better than to do that. Why are they not that smart when it comes to spiritual issues? Simply because they choose not to, and they are playing games with God.

There was a lady who worked long and hard because she valued her job. To win her boss' favour she even took on the extra task of babysitting the boss' children after work for free so that her boss could go out and socialize with her friends. She babysat the children till 10 p.m. and still had to be at work at 6am the next morning. She did that for several years and didn't think twice about it. Imagine that kind of commitment to an employer! On the other hand, it was too difficult for her to make it to church at 9:30 a.m. on Sundays! This is exactly how many Christians play games with God and with their spiritual lives, all the while letting the devil get the better of them. Nothing, and definitely not your job, should be more important than your spiritual well being.

Your Bible reading, praying, attendance in church, your spiritual life - nothing should rival that. The reason God has you down here is for His purpose, not for a job. Anyone can be laid off at a moment's notice. People put so much stock in their secular employment and put God in second place. Then they wonder why they are not blessed and why they are not prospering! The Bible says, *"seek first the kingdom of God"*. First is first! When you get up, think about God. Ask how you can be a blessing to His kingdom; how you can yield yourself better to Him. Some Christians get up and wonder how they can read as little of their Bible as possible, pray as little as possible, go to church as little as possible, and still make it to heaven! **If we are going to make it in this day and age, where the devil's works are getting meaner and meaner, it is going to be by obeying the Word of God. God must be number one!**

You can tell from the way some Christians live, that if Jesus were to physically come and visit them, they would feel very uncomfortable in His company. They think, talk and act differently from Him. If you do not have much in common with someone, you are not going to want to be around them much. The people you call your friends are the people you have things in common with. If Jesus walked into your house today, how much would you have in common with Him, or would you be miserable in His presence? Would you think He prays too much, or that He is in the spirit too much?

Rule 6: Don't make excuses, make it happen

If there are things of the flesh that are holding you back, you need to fight them and stop making excuses for yourself. It doesn't matter if it is an addiction; believe God and get free of it. Jesus died to set us free to serve Him, to do all that He has called us to do. I am not belittling the things that people experience in life, but why should a bad experience, an addiction, sickness and disease hold us down? Why should anything hinder us from fulfilling our ministry? Live your life with purpose. You are going to stand before Jesus one day and give an account of your life. Then you have eternity to spend with Him.

Ministry is as simple as helping to care for the babies in the church nursery when the need arises. You do not have to wait to be led, to feel a special leading from God. If someone offered you a "Pentecostal" handshake, containing a cheque for $2000, you won't refuse it because you do not "feel led" to take it! You would receive it and rejoice. When it comes to the things of God though many will say they do not "feel led". The Bible says we will give account for every idle word that we have said, and that includes vain words like "I don't feel led". I do not want to have to give account for words like that. I want to run my race and finish it strong! I am going for gold. I am not running my race to get silver, bronze or something less!

Rule 7: Be sure to finish your race

Let us read the words of Paul in the book of Acts chapter 20;,

> ...how I kept back nothing that was helpful, but proclaimed it to you, and taught you publicly and from house to house, testifying to Jews, and also to Greeks, repentance toward God

and faith toward our Lord Jesus Christ. And see, now I go bound in the spirit to Jerusalem, not knowing the things that will happen to me there, except that the Holy Spirit testifies in every city, saying that chains and tribulations await me. But none of these things move me; nor do I count my life dear to myself,[a] so that I may finish my race with joy, and the ministry which I received from the Lord Jesus, to testify to the gospel of the grace of God.

Acts 20:20-24

Jesus didn't save you just so you can go to heaven. If that were the case then He would have taken you there immediately after you got saved. He left you here to run your race, and to run it in such a way that you will qualify to win the prize. There are many people who run races all the time and do not finish them. It is the same spiritually. From the way some believers live it is obvious that they seem to be unaware that they are in a race. It is astounding how many of them live in disobedience and compromise, and who are offended by one person or the other. Because of offences, many won't even go to church anymore. Who has never been offended in church? Church is just like a family. In a family people sometimes hurt each other, but we should forgive one another and get over it.

Paul said: " *But none of these things move me; nor do I count my life dear to myself, so that I may finish my race with joy, and the ministry which I received from the Lord Jesus, to testify to the gospel of the grace of God.*" How are you going to share the gospel with anybody else, or help win your city for God if you are too busy being moved by every contrary thing that comes your way? It doesn't matter how much turmoil or difficulty we may have to face, we just need to be like Paul and stay focused on running our race. No opposition we encounter can compare to the glory that shall be revealed and come to us because we do what God has called us to do. There is nothing the devil can try to do to us that God cannot undo. Absolutely nothing! We know there will be difficulties, but with God's help and His grace, we can finish our race.

God has you down here for a purpose. It is only in doing that purpose that you will find joy, satisfaction, and fulfillment. Make a commitment to Him right now, and let it be from your heart. Tell Him you are going to finish your race no matter what it takes. Lay down the weights and the sin. Lay down the things that are holding you back. Bring joy to God's heart by fulfilling your ministry and His call on your life.

THE SALVATION PRAYER

If you would like to receive Jesus as your Saviour, pray the following prayer sincerely from your heart:

Dear Heavenly Father, I come to you in the name of Jesus. You said in Your word that if I confess with my mouth, "Jesus is Lord," and believe in my heart that God raised Him from the dead, I WILL BE SAVED *(Romans 10:9)*.

I do believe with my heart that Jesus Christ is the Son of God. I believe He was raised from the dead for my justification.

Your word says, "…it is with your heart that you believe and are justified, and it is with your mouth that you confess and are saved." *(Romans 10:10)*.

I do believe with my heart and I now confess with my mouth that Jesus is my Lord. Therefore, I AM SAVED!

Thank You Lord!

Congratulations on making this life changing decision, and welcome to the family of God. Please take the time to let us know that you have prayed this Salvation Prayer by contacting us online or by writing to us.

To grow in your new Christian life, it is important to study the Bible and to pray every day to your Heavenly Father.

You also need to belong to a good, Bible-based church where you can be taught the Word of God and fellowship with other believers.

I know that your Heavenly Father has a wonderful plan for you and I pray that you will experience His fullness all the days of your life, in Jesus' name.

~ Inyang Okutinyang

Contact Information

Faith Impact Ministries
a.k.a Great Lakes Faith Impact Ministries
P. O. Box 21017, RPO University Mall
Windsor, Ontario N9B 3T4
Canada

www.inyangokutinyang.com